KU-465-963

A PENGUIN SPECIAL

S215

TORTURE: CANCER OF DEMOCRACY

PIERRE VIDAL-NAQUET

TORTURE:
CANCER OF DEMOCRACY

France and Algeria 1954–62

*

PIERRE VIDAL-NAQUET

Translated by Barry Richard

PENGUIN BOOKS

Penguin Books Ltd, Harmondsworth, Middlesex
U.S.A.: Penguin Books Inc., 3300 Clipper Mill Road, Baltimore 11, Md
AUSTRALIA: Penguin Books Pty Ltd, 762 Whitehorse Road,
Mitcham, Victoria

—

First published 1963

—

Copyright © Pierre Vidal-Naquet, 1963

—

Made and printed in Great Britain
by C. Nicholls & Company Ltd
Set in Monotype Times

This book is sold subject to the condition
that it shall not, by way of trade, be lent,
re-sold, hired out, or otherwise disposed
of without the publisher's consent,
in any form of binding or cover
other than that in which
it is published

Contents

Foreword

SOME of the facts and documents quoted in this short book may seem incredible to readers who have not closely followed the development of the Algerian crisis and of French policy towards it. I want to assure the reader that I have positive proof of everything set out here; indeed I have myself collected, annotated, and published the most important of the official, secret documents dealing with torture and repression in Algeria in a thick volume entitled *La Raison d'état* (*Reasons of State*), which was published in France in April 1962 and provoked no official reaction. Any reader who wishes to study the documents used here (apart from the Wuillaume Report, which appears as an appendix to this volume) in the original will find in *La Raison d'état* the following: the reports of M. Mairey, Director-General of the Sûreté from 1954 to 1957, on the methods of repression employed by the police and the Army; the most important of the secret reports of the Safeguards Commission set up in 1957 by the Government of M. Guy Mollet; the reports of Maître Maurice Garçon and M. Robert Delavignette; one of the documents submitted to the Commission, the report of the ex-Chief of Police in Algiers, M. Paul Teitgen; notes by military commanders justifying the use of torture and summary execution; a report on the Constantine torture centre, Améziane Farm, drawn up by young soldiers and based on official information; statements by M. Reliquet, the Public Prosecutor of Algiers, and General Allard, late Commander of the Algiers Army Corps, casting doubt upon the spotlessness of the record of certain ex-ministers in the matter of the use of torture.

In view of the present situation in France, it may seem paradoxical that *La Raison d'état* could be published without provoking any denial, legal action, or special notice. But in that book the reader will also find a detailed description of how the Government kept (or failed to keep) the French people informed of what was being done in its name. Perhaps this explains why the book was allowed to be published.

Chronology

1954

7 May	Fall of Dien Bien Phu
17 June	M. Pierre Mendès-France appointed Prime Minister
20 July	Conclusion of peace in Indo-China at Geneva
August	General Cherrières Commander-in-Chief in Algeria. M. Roger Léonard remains Governor-General
1 November	Outbreak of rebellion in Algeria

1955

1 February	M. Jacques Soustelle replaces M. Léonard as Governor-General in Algeria
5 February	Fall of Mendès-France government
23 February	M. Edgar Faure Prime Minister. General Koenig (later followed by General Billotte) Minister of War. M. Maurice Bourgès-Maunoury Minister of the Interior
31 March	Government declares state of emergency
June	General Lorillot Commander-in-Chief in Algeria
20 August	Massacre of Europeans and reprisals in the north of the department of Constantine
30 September	Algeria problem raised at U.N.
2 December	Government dissolves Parliament

1956

2 January	Parliamentary elections. Appearance of 'Poujadistes'. Relative success of Republican front (alliance between Socialists, Radicals, and some ex-Gaullists)
31 January	M. Guy Mollet Prime Minister. General Catroux Resident Minister in Algeria. M. Bourgès-Maunoury Minister of National Defence. M. Mendès-France Minister of State. M. Max Lejeune Secretary of State for War
1 February	M. Soustelle fêted on leaving Algiers
6 February	Riots in Algiers greet M. Mollet. General Catroux resigns
9 February	M. Robert Lacoste Resident Minister in Algiers

12 March	Parliament votes 'special powers'
23 May	M. Mendès-France resigns as Minister of State
19 June	First execution of Moslem members of the F.L.N. in Algiers
20 June	F.L.N. attack in Algiers. Battle of Algiers begins
10 August	A bomb placed by right-wing extremists destroys a block of houses in the Casbah, causing many deaths
13 August	M. Paul Teitgen Secretary-General in charge of the general police for the prefecture of Algiers
22 October	Airliner with five F.L.N. leaders intercepted and forced to land in Algiers
13 November	General Salan Commander-in-Chief in Algeria
November –December	Evacuation of Suez
24 December	Discovery by M. Teitgen of General Faure's plot to install a military dictatorship in Algeria

1957

7 January	Decree by the super-prefect of Algiers giving police powers in Greater Algiers to General Massu, Commander of Tenth Parachute Division. M. Mollet declares his Algerian policy, reaffirming the indissolubility of the bonds between France and Algeria
16 January	Bazooka attempt on General Salan organized by the right-wing group
5 April	Commission of safeguard for individual rights and liberties set up
21 May	Fall of Mollet government
11 June	Arrest of Maurice Audin
12 June	Arrest of Henri Alleg
17 June	M. Bourgès-Maunoury Prime Minister. M. Lacoste and M. Lejeune remain. M. André Morice Minister of National Defence
21 June	Murder of Maurice Audin
12–15 July	Trial of Djamila Bouhired
12 September	Resignation of M. Teitgen after reporting the disappearance of 3,024 prisoners
24 September	Arrest of Yacef Saadi, F.L.N. leader of Algiers zone. End of battle of Algiers

30 September	*Loi-cadre* rejected by Parliament. Fall of M. Bourgès-Maunoury's Government
6 November	M. Félix Gaillard Prime Minister. M. Lacoste and M. Lejeune remain. M. Chaban-Delmas Minister of National Defence
29 November	Parliament passes *loi-cadre* (never applied)

1958

8 February	Bombing of Tunisian village of Sakhiet Sidi-Youssef. 69 civilians killed, 130 injured
27 March	Confiscation of *La Question*, by Henri Alleg
15 April	Fall of Gaillard government
26 April	Right-wing demonstrations in Algiers
13 May	Riots in Algiers. Seat of Government-General seized by Pierre Lagaillarde. M. Pierre Pflimlin Prime Minister. M. André Mutter Minister for Algeria. M. Pleven Minister of National Defence
13 May –1 June	Army takes power throughout Algeria. Formation of committees of public safety
1 June	General de Gaulle Prime Minister and Minister for Algeria. M. Pierre Guillemard Minister of National Defence
4 June	General de Gaulle's first visit to Algiers
9 June	General Salan Delegate-General in Algeria
19 September	G.P.R.A. (Algerian provisional government) formed under M. Ferhat Abbas
28 September	Adoption of new French constitution by referendum
8 October	Decree applying special powers in France
23–30 November	Parliamentary elections
12 December	M. Paul Delouvrier Delegate-General in Algeria. General Challe Commander-in-Chief (both take up appointments on 19 December)

1959

8 January	Birth of Fifth Republic. General de Gaulle President
9 January	M. Michel Debré, de Gaulle's Minister of Justice, Prime Minister. M. Guillemard remains Minister of National Defence
18 June	Publication and seizure of *La Gangrène*
16 September	General de Gaulle announces principle of self-determination
15 October	Anti-de Gaulle plot foiled

1960

18 January	General Massu recalled from Algiers after anti-de Gaulle interview
24 January	Beginning of barricades rising in Algiers. Executions of Algerians in Algiers and Oran
1 February	Surrender of Algiers mutineers. Arrest of Lagaillarde
5 February	M. Soustelle resigns. M. Pierre Messmer Minister of National Defence
3–5 March	General de Gaulle tours Algerian officer's messes, encourages Army to fight, but uses the words '*Algérie algérienne*'
30 March	General Crépin Commander-in-Chief in Algeria. General Challe Commander-in-Chief of Central European Zone of NATO
25–29 June	First official talks between French Government and Algerians at Melun end in failure
5 September	Publication of 'Declaration on the Right of Insubordination in the Algerian War', the so-called Declaration of the 121
6 September –1 October	Trial of Jeanson network before Paris military tribunal
27 October	Demonstrations in favour of peace in Algeria in Paris and provincial towns
30 November	Beginning of barricades trial
4 November	General de Gaulle uses words 'Algerian Republic'
22 November	M. Louis Joxe Minister of State for Algeria
24 November	M. Jean Morin Delegate-General in Algiers
9–13 December	European demonstrations followed by Moslem demonstrations in Algiers

1961

8 January	Referendum in France approving self-determination
25 January	General Challe asks to retire
1 February	General Gambiez Commander-in-Chief in Algeria
2 March	End of barricades trial. All accused present acquitted
31 March	Assassination of Mayor of Évian by O.A.S.
22 April	*Putsch* in Algiers. Generals Challe, Zeller, and Jouhaud, later joined by General Salan, take power. O.A.S. attacks in Paris
25 April	Collapse of *putsch*

20 May	Beginning of Évian talks. Cancellation of all offensive operations by the French Army
29 May	Generals Challe and Zeller condemned to fifteen years' imprisonment
7 June	General Ailleret Commander-in-Chief in Algeria
27 August	M. Benyoussef Ben Khedda replaces M. Ferhat Abbas as President of the G.P.R.A.
17–18 October	Algerian demonstrations in Paris against curfew. Many Algerians killed
2 November	Hunger strike by Algerian prisoners in France starts
19 December	Anti-O.A.S. demonstrations in Paris
1962	
16 January	Three officers accused of torturing acquitted by Paris military tribunal
8 February	Anti-O.A.S. demonstrations in Paris. Eight Parisians killed at Métro station Charonne
10 February	French and Algerian ministers meet near Swiss frontier
18 March	Évian agreements end war in Algeria
22 March	Amnesty decrees for Algerians and members of French forces of law and order for acts in Algeria
26 March	European demonstrations in Algiers
8 April	Évian agreements approved by referendum in France
15 April	Amnesty decree for Algerians and members of French forces of law and order for acts in France
20 April	Ex-General Salan, head of O.A.S., arrested in Algiers. Succeeded by M. Georges Bidault. General Fourquet Commander-in-Chief in Algeria
15 May	Beginning of trial of ex-General Salan
23 May	General Salan allowed mitigating circumstances and condemned to life imprisonment
7 June	Two members of O.A.S. executed near Paris
17 June	Local agreements between Algerians and European leaders in Algiers
1 July	Referendum in Algeria on self-determination and independence

CHAPTER 1

Introductory

CAN a great nation, liberal by tradition, allow its institutions, its army, and its system of justice to degenerate over the span of a few years as a result of the use of torture, and by its concealment and deception of such a vital issue call the whole Western concept of human dignity and the rights of the individual into question? That is the question which I wish to discuss in this book.

It is now common knowledge in the West that, throughout most of the recent war in Algeria, France made general use of the practices of torture, summary execution, and large-scale deportation. It is also known that many of these habits have overflowed into France itself, and at the moment of writing there seems little likelihood that the end of this situation is in sight. The part played by torture throughout the Algerian war can be summed up in a few words; it started as a police method of interrogation, developed into a military method of operation, and then ultimately turned into a clandestine State institution which struck at the very roots of the life of the nation.

Can an institution be clandestine? The noun and the adjective scarcely seem compatible. Nevertheless, since the torturers were not isolated individuals acting according to their personal whims, torture did in fact become an institution. No doubt there were many cases of individual action both before and in the early days of the Algerian war; for first police officers and then later on military commanders were quick to assume a heavy load of personal responsibility; but from January 1957 onwards they were all acting on orders. Although at a later stage some ministers tried to put the brake on, by then they could do nothing. The torturers had good reason to feel that they were acting within legal bounds. The fact that some of them may have gone well beyond their instructions out of sadism or a spirit of initiative, is a difference of degree, not of kind. The institution was, moreover,

15

clandestine. No decree reestablishing the Middle Ages post of executioner is to be found in the *Journal Officiel* of the French Republic, nor is any vote for the purchase of instruments of torture to be found in any budget passed by the National Assembly. In general only verbal orders were given; none the less they resulted in the setting up of a torture service. Thus the State itself built up a clandestine State which one day would attempt to destroy it.

It may well sound implausible to speak of a clandestine institution when every conceivable type of account has been published. There have been accounts by the victims, the best known but by no means the only one being *La Question* by Henri Alleg;* then there is an apologia for torture, *La Guerre moderne*, by Colonel Trinquier, one of those principally responsible for the maintenance of order in Algiers in 1957; and there have been accounts by young soldiers, showing that their duties in Algeria included being present at or taking part in 'interrogations'. As well as all these, there have been accounts by Parisians who live near those places, not far from the Élysée Palace (the official residence of the President), where Algerian students were tortured in December 1959, or who saw Algerians being drowned in the Seine in the late summer and autumn of 1961. But one of the most disturbing symptoms of this French affliction is that facts which ought to be obvious to anyone who takes the trouble to keep himself properly informed, are still to a great extent unknown to the general public; even the most superficial sounding of public opinion would reveal that the majority of Frenchmen are almost completely ignorant of the fact that, during the Algerian war, torture developed into an institution. Many of those who served in Algeria merely led barrack-room life there and never came in contact with the realities of the war; many, too, when they returned to France did their best to forget the shameful events which they had seen.

Racial feeling has reached such a pitch that the average Frenchman is incapable of 'putting himself in the place' of an Algerian who was tortured, or shot after a mockery of a trial, or summarily executed. It can be argued that this was a savage war and that

* Henri Alleg, *The Question*, John Calder, London, 1958.

the enemy employed equally disgusting methods. But it is worth looking at the preface (by the publisher, Jérôme Lindon) of a book by a young Algerian, Djamal Amrani,* written in 1960:

How many Frenchmen, as they go on accepting the horrors practised in Algeria without protest and with the soothing thought that 'the other side started it' reflect that one day this sort of argument may come true and rebound upon them; that one day the small boys who are electrocuted, the girls who are raped, and the people who are murdered 'while attempting to escape' may be called not Djamal or Djamila, but simply Jean or Jeanne; that they might, in fact, be their own children.

A short example will perhaps show how incapable the average French are of putting themselves in the place of others – perhaps one of the most serious lessons of these dreadful years. At dawn on 7 June 1962 two O.A.S. killers were shot in one of the forts of Paris for having murdered a Superintendent of Police in Algiers. Commenting upon this *France-Soir*, which has the largest circulation of any French daily newspaper, wrote:

The last executions of political prisoners in Paris took place on 23 May 1954. On that day three Gestapo torturers were executed by a firing squad in the fort of Vincennes.

France-Soir had completely forgotten that many Algerians, some as late as December 1960, had been guillotined in the courtyard of the Santé prison after legal proceedings which were indubitably political in character. What this shows is that, although up to the referendum of 1 July 1962 an Algerian was legally a citizen of France, he was not a Frenchman, and that in the eyes of many Frenchmen, including many of those responsible for forming French public opinion, he was not even a human being. However in the closing months of the Algerian war a certain number of Europeans who were members or supporters of the O.A.S. were tortured in their turn. Several newspapers, which up to that time had referred only to 'supposed victims of torture' or the 'tortured', with the words carefully printed in inverted commas, abruptly discovered that torture really did exist. Yet few took advantage of this opportunity to look back into the past and reconsider the implications.

* Djamal Amrani, *Le Témoin*, Éditions de Minuit, Paris, 1960.

In this book I shall necessarily be dealing largely with Algeria and the war in Algeria. However, I believe it would be a mistake to establish too clear and direct a relationship of cause and effect between the Algerian war and the practice of torture. It is true that the vast majority of those who have been victims of 'interrogation by torture' during recent years have been tortured for reasons connected with events in Algeria. It is also true that the nature of the war in Algeria made the use of torture almost inevitable, as will become only too apparent. But the real question goes far deeper than the Algerian problem. Torture was used in France long before the outbreak of the war in Algeria and it will probably be used in France again. The one can therefore hardly be regarded as the 'consequence of the other', just as the use of torture in Algeria was not merely a 'consequence' of its use during the Nazi occupation, as the superficial saying goes.

This book is intended for readers outside France, and it must always be remembered that there is not a single country, not even the most liberal in the world, which is safe from the infection whose symptoms I am about to describe, or which can be certain of being able to disentangle itself from a chain of events similar to that with which I shall be dealing.

Torture was for centuries a legal, normal, and commonplace institution in France.* Many writers on law have pointed out that it stemmed from the old provisions of Roman law against *crimen majestatis*, or crimes against the State, to which were later added crimes against the Church, and that its practice was reintroduced into the West at the end of the eleventh century. The practice was gradually codified; differing degrees of torture were laid down. There was the *ordinary* interrogation, and the *extraordinary* interrogation; there was also the *preparatory* interrogation, intended to make a prisoner come to terms with the truth; there was the *preliminary* interrogation used before an execution in order to make a man whose guilt had been established give away the names of his accomplices. Torture was inflicted by a public servant, the executioner, who was also responsible for carrying out executions. It took place in a special chamber in the

* See Alec Mellor, *La Torture* (second edition), 1961.

18

place of detention and was invariably carried out in the presence of magistrates who took down the confession of the suspect or guilty person. From the seventeenth century onwards, during the period of absolutist monarchies, an 'abolitionist' current of opinion against the practice developed. This was a feature common to all Western European countries, including even Russia, and the best-known exposition of it is the Italian Beccaria's *On Crimes and Punishments*. This book was published in 1764 and was immediately translated into twenty-two European languages.* The arguments used by the abolitionists of that time are identical with those which have reappeared today, but in those days they were new arguments and they played an essential part in the growth of modern liberalism. Torture, it was said, is *inhuman;* it is also inefficient; it is frequently used against innocent people and the confessions extracted by it have no validity. Beccaria summed up the problem with sarcasm:

The strength of the muscles and the sensitivity of the nerves of an innocent person being known factors, the problem is to find the level of suffering necessary to make him confess to any given crime.

Torture may have had its enemies, but it also had its friends. Nevertheless it was abolished in two stages by Louis XVI; the 'preparatory' interrogation in 1780 and the 'preliminary' interrogation in 1788. At the beginning of the Revolution a decree of 8 October 1789, put a final end to the practice; previously a declaration of 26 August 1789 had laid down that 'security', which included the inviolability of the person, was one of the 'rights of man'. Article 9 of the Declaration stated:

Any man is presumed to be innocent until he has been found guilty; in the event therefore of his arrest being considered essential, any act of violence other than that necessary to assure his detention must be severely punished by law.

It is important to note that this was not a question of a political right, but of an 'inalienable, unalterable, and sacred' right. Under the Revolution heads fell, sometimes in somewhat doubtful circumstances, but torture was never used. Article 303 of the

* In France, Voltaire wrote the preface to the translation. In England, Jeremy Bentham became the apostle of the views of this Italian philosopher.

French Penal Code, which was drafted under the Consulate when many highwaymen were still in the habit of 'warming up' the feet of their victims in order to make them give away where their fortunes were held, is still in force and lays down:

Any criminal, whatever his status, who in committing his crime uses torture or commits acts of barbarism, will be punished as if he were guilty of murder [i.e. *will be subject to the death penalty*].

The abolitionist view, which had won the day in many European countries before it did so in France, seemed finally to have gained a world-wide victory in 1948, when the General Assembly of the United Nations adopted a 'universal declaration on the rights of man'. Article 5 of this declaration lays down 'no man will be subjected to torture or to cruel, inhuman, or degrading punishment or treatment'. Moreover the preamble to this declaration recalls that 'disregard or contempt for the rights of man has resulted in acts of barbarism which revolt the conscience of humanity'. Clearly, 184 years after Beccaria had written *On Crimes and Punishment* the problem was still with us.

What was the French attitude towards torture in 1954, immediately before the outbreak of the war in Algeria?

Had the ordinary Frenchman of that time been asked this question, he probably would have made an immediate reference to the Gestapo. In fact throughout the last war this organization, or, to give it its proper title, the Fourth Bureau of the Reichssicherheitshauptamt, had once more made torture a recognized institution; Himmler's instructions to his agents laid down that torture was to be employed. However, the word Gestapo was also used inaccurately in France to describe the German Counter-Intelligence Service, the Abwehr. This organization worked in a more orthodox manner and refused to allow its own members to use torture on those under detention, delegating the job to agents recruited in the occupied territories, who were universally despised, even by those who employed them.

When the liberation came, a number of accounts were published of the methods of torture in vogue, particularly on the water torture, which is rightly considered to have been popularized, if not invented, by a Belgian Abwehr agent, Masuy, who was later executed. Although the police who had been in the service of the Vichy state or of the Germans in general were let off, those who had actually handed over their fellow countrymen to be tortured were in many cases sentenced to death.

Though everybody displayed righteous indignation at these practices, the general feeling was that torture was a characteristically foreign institution and that in France, whose institutions were founded upon the rights of man, there had been no case of torture since 1789 and that there would be none after 1945. Both suppositions were wrong.

Although to all intents and purposes there was no torture in Western Europe during the nineteenth century, it had in fact never entirely disappeared. Nor, as we shall see, did the liberation of France bring about its disappearance.* This does not of course mean that torture had become a common feature of life in France. But both in France, and still more in the French colonies, the practice of torture continued, underground and outside the legal system, the existence of such practices being taken seriously by very few Frenchmen, unfortunately.

Does this mean that torture had become endemic in France? Yes – at any rate in so far as certain specialized counter-espionage sections of the police were concerned, as, for instance, the Directions de la Sécurité du Territoire (D.S.T.). Detailed reports prove that this organization used the electrical torture in certain instances in 1949. A much more common habit was to 'beat up' a suspect who had been summoned to police headquarters as a 'witness'. On several occasions these 'beatings-up' ended in death; for example, a scrap dealer who was suspected of being a receiver of stolen goods was beaten to death in Bordeaux in 1949. Years later his murderers were brought before an assize court and acquitted.

* The truth rapidly became apparent to those who wanted to see it. During and after the liberation a certain number of collaborators were in their turn tortured. Although this was not a systematic development, the fact remains that cases did occur and to their credit some members of the Resistance forbade or denounced such goings-on.

In March 1955 a civil Inspector-General wrote:

There are certain police practices which although *generally accepted* are nevertheless tantamount to violence. For example: a prolonged interrogation which relies for its results on the physical exhaustion of the prisoner; refusal to allow the prisoner food, drink, and tobacco, while superintendents and inspectors smoke, drink, and eat in front of him; or merely threats and intimidation.

In his book *Traité théorique et pratique de police judiciaire* (*The Theory and Practice of Criminal Police Procedures*) which came out in 1945, M. Louis Lambert, an instructor at the National Police College, dealt with the theory behind these practices and called them by their true name 'licensed torture'. The phrase gave rise to great indignation and was expunged from subsequent editions of the book. The practices themselves, however, aroused no similar indignation.

The trouble is that the French penal system is to some extent poisoned at its roots. The system of preliminary hearings before trial is legally inconsistent. Once a trial begins the prosecution and defence are on an equal footing in law, but the preliminary hearing is carried out in secret, and, moreover, the police have the right to detain any individual arrested for twenty-four hours before bringing him before a magistrate. This provision was originally laid down in order to give country gendarmes time to bring a suspect before a tribunal in the nearest town. But in our own time the police have used this period in order to carry out a full-scale preliminary investigation, of which the essential feature is a determination to extract a confession at all costs. The moment a confession has been obtained the suspect becomes the accused. The average examining magistrate takes little trouble to find out *how* the confession had been obtained and considers his duty to be primarily that of ratifying the confession which has already been made to the police.

No one protested much against these procedures so long as they were only applied to ordinary criminals. The accused knew that he would only make his case worse if he lodged a complaint against the police and that in any case no one would believe him; indeed it never occurred to him to complain, since once in the hands of the police he scarcely expected to be treated differently.

The result was a deplorable conspiracy of silence between criminals and the police, with the victims tacitly agreeing that such practices remain 'under cover'. Of course, if the victims happened to be innocent or upper class people that was another matter. Even then their complaints seldom achieved very much. Moreover the police hit upon an extremely convenient procedure: anyone who, while in the hands of the police, announced that he intended to make a complaint of ill-treatment, discovered that in addition he was now charged with 'recalcitrance'. In any event it had long been the accepted practice that a member of the police force should never be sentenced by a court of law. An Inspectorate General of Police Services had the duty of ensuring that this particular dirty linen was not washed in public. As a result the vast majority of complaints brought against the police ended in the files of the Inspectorate General of Police Services, a fact of which I have had personal experience.

The next question is whether torture had become endemic in the French Colonies. Here examples are both more numerous and more serious for obvious reasons. In colonial territories the 'natives' are directly subject to the machinery of oppression and no guarantee of protection for the individual can be furnished by the Press, the judicial system, and public opinion which normally fulfil this vital role in Western countries. The victims are not criminals or suspects, but the entire mass of the population unwilling to submit to regimentation by the machinery of colonial government. Racial prejudice also increases the torturers' feelings of impunity. Torture was a feature of the conquest of Algeria between 1830 and 1871; and has since been used whenever there has been a crisis in the colonial system.

In a courageous piece of reporting entitled *Indo-China S.O.S.* published in 1935, Andrée Viollis described the tortures to which political opponents of France, both men and women, were subjected in the police establishments in Cholon – and shows that the electrical torture was already in use at that time. She was a journalist who went with a commission of inquiry led by M. Paul Reynaud, then the Minister for the Colonies. At the end of the visit Reynaud asked her to go on keeping him informed, knowing full well that his staff would only show him what it wanted him to see. He returned convinced of the wonderful work being done by France in Indo-China and, in spite of Andrée Viollis, was never informed of the sufferings of some of the inhabitants.

The war in Indo-China broke out eleven years later and it was the first subversive war with which the French Army had to deal. During the war torture was employed, unsystematically perhaps, but very widely nevertheless.* A journalist who visited Indo-China at this time gives the following account of a meeting with a French officer in his quarters:

'Here is my desk,' said the officer, 'my table, my typewriter, my wash-basin, and over there in the corner my machine for making people talk.' When I obviously failed to understand what he was driving at, he added, 'The dynamo, I mean. Very handy for interrogating prisoners! You attach the positive pole and the negative pole, turn the handle, and the prisoner squeals.'†

Although these were grave facts, they did not constitute a national problem. No conscripts served in the war in Indo-China. Moreover, the Indo-Chinese war was extremely unpopular in France itself, and the French judicial system therefore had no need to cover the practice of torture in Indo-China with the mantle of its authority.

This was not the case, unfortunately, in Madagascar. On 29 March 1947 a rebellion broke out in the island and 150 Frenchmen were killed. The local authorities wrongly laid responsibility for these events at the door of the Mouvement Démocratique de la Rénovation Malgache (M.D.R.M.), the Nationalist party which had won the recent elections. The repression was bloody. The leaders of the M.D.R.M. were arrested *en masse* and variously tortured in the presence of the Director of the Sûreté, M. Baron. This rapidly became public knowledge, but it seemed almost inconceivable at that time. The object was to compel those under arrest to endorse the administration's theory of the background to the revolt. A trial took place in the criminal court at

* According to Paul Mus, late director of the French school of Archaeology in Hanoi, recently one of the negotiators with Ho-Chi-Minh and a Professor in France, one of the officers who was opposed to the use of torture was Colonel Massu!

† *Témoignage chrétien*, 29 July 1949.

Tananarive, capital of Madagascar, from 22 July to 4 October 1948. The accused were able to prove their innocence conclusively and stated that their confessions had been extracted from them by torture. The trial itself, although following the correct legal forms, was a classic example of a miscarriage of justice; for instance the most important witness was executed three days before the trial opened. In spite of all this, the verdict was six death sentences and ten sentences of ten years or more of prison or forced labour.

The various tortures that had been inflicted on the accused were described in great detail in the National Assembly on 22 September 1948. The Minister for French Overseas Territories, M. Coste-Floret, did not deny the evidence, stating, 'I believe that violence has been used. The possibility of this is one of the defects of semi-official interrogations.' He tried to minimize the whole affair by quoting a letter from an officer which said: 'We must not talk of torture at every turn, if only out of respect for those who really have been tortured.' No inquiry was ever opened nor was any action ever taken against the torturers. M. Baron merely resigned and reappeared as a member of the board of a large financial concern in Tananarive.*

Even more significant is the fact that this verdict was confirmed by the French Supreme Court, the Cour de Cassation, whose duty it is, when appealed to by those sentenced, to pronounce whether the provisions of the law have been adhered to. Counsel for the Defence was able to offer incontrovertible proof that both the letter and the spirit of the law had been broken. In spite of this, on 29 July 1949 one of the prosecution counsel asked the Court whether a certain article of the criminal code was intended 'to be adhered to as strictly in what used to be called the young colonies, now grouped under the heading of overseas territories integrated in the French Union, as it is in France.'† This was a clear example of 'reasons of state', all the more significant and disquieting when it is remembered that in 1899 and again in 1906 it was the Cour de Cassation which ultimately saw justice done in the Dreyfus affair. The highest

---

* Of which he is still Chairman.

† The whole Madagascan affair is most clearly and objectively dealt with in Pierre Stibbes's book, *Justice pour les Malgaches*, Paris, 1954.

authorities of the state were accomplices in the Madagascar affair. With our present hindsight it is clear that this was nothing less than a dress rehearsal for the events which were to take place in Algeria.

Algeria was obviously likely to present grave problems for other reasons too, for it occupied a special position in the 1954 French colonial system. In the way that English children had for generations looked upon Ireland as an extension of Great Britain, French children, from their school and college days, had been taught that Algeria was merely an extension of metropolitan France. And indeed the million or so 'French of Algeria', who included Frenchmen by birth, naturalized Frenchmen, and the Jews who had been given French nationality by the Crémieux decree in 1871, did constitute a complete, undeniably French society in Algeria. In comparison with them the nine million Muslims were at best only second-rate citizens. The relationship between this colonial society and the State of France was complex in the extreme. The French of Algeria regarded it as their right that the Mother Country should preserve their privileged position in its entirety. This status had been established by force and maintained by police methods, including, if necessary, torture. 'This is the day of the gendarme in North Africa,' wrote the main settler newspaper, the *Écho d'Alger*, after the start of the insurrection of 8 May 1945 – which was put down exactly as the settlers demanded. To some extent the settlers were able to police Algeria themselves, and could therefore snap their fingers at France. Like many of the British settlers in Kenya, some on several occasions threatened to set up an independent State. Their final fling came at the very end of the Algerian war, during the O.A.S. period.

For her part France has made several attempts to divorce herself from the settlers, the first in the reign of Napoleon III who, to the fury of the settlers, styled himself king of an 'Arab Kingdom'. But France could not divorce herself from the theory which she herself propounded – that of 'French Algeria'. Whenever a Governor-General incurred the displeasure of the settlers, he was immediately recalled, so that 'French Algeria' could again become what it had in fact always been, the creation and the creature of the 'French in Algeria'.

It was logical therefore, that any challenge to French sovereignty in Algeria should be treated as a problem of internal rather than external politics, and should involve the use of the whole machinery of the State and the full forces of the nation. There could be only one result. The willingness to use any means, even torture, was bound to lead to a totalitarian system.

It is clear from all this that, on the eve of the Algerian insurrection there was no organization within the French state capable of resisting the police or the army if they decided upon a systematic use of torture. That is not to say that there were not a great many who acted honourably and in good faith. For example both M. Jean Mairey, who in his capacity of Director-General of the Sûreté, was head of the French police force from 16 July 1954, and was personally opposed to the use of torture in interrogation; and the Government of M. Mendès-France which came into power on 17 June 1954, realized the danger implicit in allowing certain branches of the police to become to all intents and purposes autonomous, and dismissed M. Baylot, the powerful Chief of Police of the Paris Préfecture. Nevertheless the machinery of government had already been poisoned at home and was positively gangrenous in the colonies.

In the modern world the machine of state is not, as it was to some extent in the nineteenth century, a mere thin crust over the structure of society, susceptible to the smallest movement of public opinion. As long ago as the end of the last century the Dreyfus affair had shown that the Secret Service, and the General Staff which backed it with its authority, were indeed a State within the State and would not hesitate to use any method, however disreputable, to keep an innocent man in prison if his reinstatement seemed likely to lead to an inquiry into those methods. Today it is not merely a question of the secret service or the General Staff. In every Western nation the State has become a gigantic machine which controls every important aspect of the life of the country. In France it is even master of those modern information services (radio and television) which are pushing the normal Press into the background.

On 13 January 1898 the paper *L'Aurore*, in the course of a few hours, distributed 300,000 copies of an issue which included an article by Émile Zola entitled 'J'Accuse'. This was an exposé of the truth in the Dreyfus affair and the effect it produced was enormous. However, the day has passed when a Press campaign could put an end to a scandal or bring down a régime. If it were to have the same effect today, 'J'Accuse' would have to be televised. But French television is controlled by the State, and the State is not in the habit of making accusations against itself. Thus, when a body which is part of the machinery of the State is involved in a crime like that of torture, it is the whole State system which is in the dock and it is the whole machinery of the State which becomes an accomplice of the crime if it tries to cover up the truth.

CHAPTER 2

Torture and the Police

DURING the night of 31 October–1 November 1954 a number of incidents of varying gravity occurred all over Algeria – assassinations, attacks on military and police establishments, and acts of sabotage. At the same time tracts were distributed reproducing a manifesto signed by an organization which until then was not even known to exist – the F.L.N. (Front de Libération Nationale – National Liberation Front). Only much later was it realized that this was the start of an insurrection challenging the authority, and indeed the presence, of the French in Algeria.

At this time the official doctrine on justice and the police in Algeria could be summed up in a formula endlessly repeated by those in power – 'Algeria is part of France'. But this doctrine was not as old-established as might be supposed; the principle of the equality of all men before the common law was not established until 7 March 1944 when a decree to that effect was issued at Algiers by the 'French Committee of National Liberation'. Before that date, an oppressive, rapid, and summary legal system applied to certain categories of crime, but was used only against the Muslim population. Still Algiers, Oran, and Constantine, the capital towns of the three departments, had courts of law properly constituted according to the French legal code. There was in law no distinction between the Public Prosecutor of the Court of Appeal of Algiers, who was head of the machinery of repression, and his counterpart in, say, Riom or Aix-en-Provence. It needed no great flight of fancy for Albert Camus, who was born in Oran, to depict in his famous novel *L'Étranger* (*The Outsider*) a European sentenced to death and executed for the murder of a Muslim. Justice was the justice of France. But even this was for the Muslims the justice of a ruling class and of foreigners – principles alone are not enough. The vast majority of the magistrates were locally recruited from among Algerian

French, whereas for a Muslim it was difficult even to become clerk of the court, a post little sought after and of scant influence. The public prosecutor of Algiers, M. Susini, was rightly considered to be one of the leaders of the Algerian lobby which represented the views of the extreme *colons*.

And the police? In Algiers there was a Directorate General of Public Safety in Algiers immediately subordinate to the French Ministry of the Interior. The criminal code, which lays down that no man may be detained for more than twenty-four hours without being brought before a magistrate, was in force in Algeria. We have already seen the use to which this rule was put in France; there was no question of its observance in Algeria. In October 1949 M. Naegelen, the Governor-General of Algeria, wrote in an official circular (which remained a dead letter): '. . . strong-arm techniques must be absolutely prohibited as a method of investigation. I am determined to punish with the utmost severity not only those members of the public service found guilty of using violence but also their superiors.' This shows that the problem was known to exist.

A young French historian, Robert Bonnaud, who was called up for military service in Algeria in 1956, painted the following picture of one of his companions:

My friend J. M., a native of Martinique and a sensitive, sickly, and slightly neurotic young man, explained to us one day why he hated his father. His father was a policeman who had spent many years in North Africa. M.'s first memories were of his father torturing men in the grilling-hot courtyard of some Algerian police station. The unfortunate boy always pictured his father's face against a background of swollen lips, bleeding noses, and bloodshot eyes. In his mind he could barely separate his father's voice from the cries of his victims.

In spite of such official circulars as M. Naegelen's, the effect of any charges of violence brought forward was negligible and aroused little interest in official circles. M. Fonlupt-Esperaber, a Christian Democrat, who had been a Prefect and a member of the Conseil d'État (the highest administrative court), said one day in the National Assembly: 'In 1950 (I have documents to prove this) eighty complaints of acts of torture were laid before the public prosecutor. I have no evidence that these complaints produced the smallest result.'

Even if the government had wished to take the police of Algeria in hand, it could hardly have done so because of the extremely antiquated organization of the force. It was more like a network of private police forces than a national one. Its officers felt that they were servants not of the Governor-General, who was the head of the administration, but of the prefects and sub-prefects or even of local associations presided over by big wine growers or gentlemen farmers. Even when these cliques were rent by internal squabbles they would still close their ranks if the racial supremacy of the European over the Muslim were questioned. The worst feature of the system was that this ill-organized police force was armed with powers unknown to the police in France; for example, the prison service, which in France is under the Ministry of Justice, was in Algeria under the police. In other words Muslims were arrested and often tortured by the police, brought before courts which were both biased and permeated with a spirit of racialism, and finally, after being sentenced, passed into the hands of a prison service which itself was subordinate to the police. The whole process took place within a closed circuit of which torture formed an integral part. The system was the same for both political detainees and common law criminals. Colette and Francis Jeanson gave an accurate picture of Algeria in 1954 when they called a book, which first appeared shortly after the beginning of the insurrection, *L'Algérie hors-la-loi* (*Algeria the Outlaw*). In short Algeria was a police state ruled by anarchy and tyranny, where the anarchy merely made the tyranny inefficient.

We must next consider whether the outbreak of the insurrection changed this state of affairs.

When the war in Algeria began, there were certain operations which were at once entrusted to the army – and in particular to the parachute troops brought back from Indo-China after the conclusion of the Geneva treaty with the Viet-Minh in July 1954. But the repression of both town and countryside was essentially the business of the police, and the *gendarmerie*. Using out-of-date lists of suspects the police systematically arrested members of the Algerian nationalist organization known as the Mouvement pour le Triomphe des Libertés Démocratiques (Movement for the Triumph of Democratic Liberties). This organization was itself in a state of upheaval at the time and so had nothing to do with the insurrection. Yet a number of those arrested were subjected to the vilest tortures.

Surprisingly the facts were very soon known in France. As early as 15 January 1955 *L'Express*, a weekly review generally known to have close connexions with Pierre Mendès-France, then Prime Minister, published an article by François Mauriac entitled (prophetically) 'La Question' ('Torture').* It soon leaked out that men were being dragged, still bleeding, from police quarters to the offices of examining magistrates; that legal advisers were being prevented from communicating with their clients; and that police doctors were signing certificates to prove that such and such a prisoner was in perfect health when his lawyer could affirm that 'his back was covered with open or barely healed wounds'. Many such cases were brought to the notice of the National Assembly during a debate on the Algerian problem which took place from 2–5 February – and not only by Muslim members, (who it should be noted, were in fact *nominated* by the Administration) but also by deputies of the centre, left, and extreme left.

What was the reaction in official circles? The Minister of the Interior, M. Mitterrand, was evasive. While he admitted that certain excesses had taken place, he insisted on paying a solemn tribute to the Algerian police. M. Mendès-France was far more definite; he paid tribute to François Mauriac and spoke of 'horrible excesses which have at times been committed; they may have been exaggerated in certain instances, I admit, but they must stop everywhere and at once.' This was the first and last time that such language was used by a man in an official position and in an official assembly. But M. Mendès-France's government did not survive this passage of arms. It fell a few hours later, at dawn on 5 February.

* At the same time Claude Bourdet, writing in *France-Observateur*, violently denounced what he called 'your Gestapo in Algeria'.

Had any steps in fact been taken? M. Mendès-France did not take legal action against those police officers who had used torture. It is hard to say how far this might have been possible but it was the only effective measure that could have been applied. Instead he took administrative action, announcing that he intended to transfer a certain number of suspect police officers from Algeria to France and to *integrate* the police of Algeria with the police of France, which was under less suspicion of using these methods. In addition he decided to get the facts. The Minister of the Interior seconded to the new Governor-General, M. Jacques Soustelle (at the time still considered a man of liberal outlook), a civil Inspector-General (one of the most senior Civil Servants in the French hierarchy), M. Roger Wuillaume, a man, as M. Mitterrand publicly affirmed, of 'complete moral integrity'. M. Wuillaume's task was to inform M. Soustelle whether violence had been used, if so, how serious it was, and to propose measures to put an end to it. M. Wuillaume's inquiry, like all French Civil Service inquiries, was intended to be strictly secret.

M. Mendès-France had little chance of purging and integrating the Algerian police, as his Government fell almost immediately after his programme had been announced, and M. Edgar Faure's Government, which succeeded, only partly implemented the programme it had inherited. Even so there was an immediate chorus of protest drawing attention to the danger: the French police was all too prone to use illegal methods, particularly in Paris: would it not be contaminated with the methods employed in Algeria? The intention was to 'metropolitanize' the Algerian police; but was there not a risk of 'Algerianizing' the police of France? This forecast proved all too true, as we shall see later; for the police officers who were transferred from Algeria to France formed 'activist' groups which became 'torture' cells.

M. Wuillaume's inquiry was a much more serious affair. He submitted his report* to M. Soustelle on 2 March 1955. M. Wuillaume had restricted his inquiry to the Kabylie and to the area of Constantine, but he rightly considered that he had sufficient information. He had worked scientifically; he had interrogated police officers, who were most disturbed by his inquiry,

* See Appendix.

and no fewer than sixty-one prisoners who had been carefully chosen from among those most unlikely to have been urged by their lawyers to make complaints. His conclusions were clear: physical violence of every type had been inflicted on suspects throughout Algeria. M. Wuillaume gave a list (which it is not proposed to reproduce here); it ranges from detention well beyond the twenty-four-hour limit – at times up to fifteen or twenty days – to almost indescribable strong-arm methods including a general use of the water and electrical tortures. He found, also, that this violence was an 'old-established practice' dating back to well before the Algerian war. According to the police officers interrogated, it was the result of the stubborn resistance which Muslims put up to the normal methods of interrogation, and it was practised by 'all the police forces' – the *gendarmerie*, the criminal police (subordinate to the magistrates), and even the 'general information service', which really only existed to provide the government with confidential information on the attitude of the population, but which nevertheless used torture 'in spite of the fact that their offices were so small'. The magistrates were in fact accomplices, since they did not insist on medical examination, even of those prisoners who showed the most obvious effects of ill-treatment. But M. Wuillaume added that these excesses had produced results in that they had helped to uncover several underground organizations.

M. Wuillaume's description of conditions in Algeria is entirely objective, and his conclusions are equally clear. He was very struck by the uneasiness which his inquiry caused among the police, who maintained that they would be paralysed if they were not allowed to use torture. Although M. Wuillaume proposed certain exemplary punishments (for instance of two inspectors, both Muslims however), he considered it unwise to make a general attempt to track down the culprits and even recommended a number of police officers for decorations in order to boost morale. He advised that the most serious cruelties be stopped but that the police must not be made impotent.

We must have the courage to take action on this difficult problem. Either we must adhere to the hypocritical attitude which has been the rule up to the present, which consists in turning a blind eye to what the police are doing, provided that no signs of the cruelties administered remain and nothing can be proven; although this may cause excesses from time to time, the police would carry on with their own job with the authorities as tacit accomplices. Or alternatively we must assume an attitude of false indignation and pretend that we have been deceived, heap anathema on the heads of the police, forbid any methods of interrogation other than those which are strictly legal, and thereby plunge the police into a state of disorder and paralysis.

To solve this dilemma M. Wuillaume put forward his solution. According to the experts

... the water and electricity methods, provided they are carefully used, produce a shock which is more psychological than physical and do not therefore constitute excessive cruelty. ... The criminal police, and only the criminal police, should be authorized ... to use 'special methods' ... employed only in the presence of an officer or superintendent of criminal police. This conclusion, which takes us back to a recent and painful past [a reference to the Gestapo] may appear repugnant. But since the problem is with us, we must face it.

The gravity of M. Wuillaume's conclusions scarcely requires emphasis. A highly placed Civil Servant, in no way connected with the police, proposed simply to legalize torture, to re-establish what in the Middle Ages was known as 'interrogation by water', adding also a more modern method, electricity. As a result of his contact with the police M. Wuillaume had given birth to a doctrine. We shall see that it was later to be taken up in almost identical terms by the military.

But what was the attitude of M. Soustelle, to whom the report was addressed? In a note, of which I have seen the original, M. Soustelle 'categorically refused' to agree with M. Wuillaume's conclusions about the use of the water and electrical tortures. He did however accept the part of the report which in retrospect may appear the most important: the recommendation to make no attempt to track down those responsible for the use of such methods before 1 March 1955. It was therefore agreed that although torture remained theoretically forbidden the torturers were still to be protected by higher authority. Of all possible solutions the one chosen was the most hypocritical.

M. Wuillaume's conclusions were in principle supposed to

apply only to Algeria, but the problems he raised were shortly afterwards to be faced in France, at the higher level of the government itself.

On 20 March 1955 M. Faure's Government received a detailed report on the work of the police in Algeria prepared by the Director of the Sûreté, M. Jean Mairey. M. Mairey, who occupied this post from 16 July 1954 to 19 August 1957, was a police officer neither by profession nor inclination. Originally a university teacher of history and geography, he was, like M. Michel Debré and M. Bourgès-Maunoury, one of a number of senior Civil Servants and politicians thrown up by the Resistance. Like many of the prefects he was a member of the Socialist Party. His attitude to the Algerian insurrection was in many respects that of the average Frenchman. He believed that the rebels were fanatics inspired by Colonel Nasser; he did not distinguish between the F.L.N. and Messali Hadj's M.N.A. (Mouvement National Algérien – Algerian National Movement); he gave first priority to the re-establishment of order, or as M. Soustelle began to call it, 'pacification'. The problems set out in his report are therefore primarily technical. Instead of the efficient centralized instrument that every senior Civil Servant has had a right to expect since the Napoleonic era, he found the Algerian police to be more like a hotch-potch of private armies.

He felt that the problem of violence (which he was the first to bring forcefully to the attention of those responsible – by passing on the Wuillaume report to the government with an indignant comment) was intimately connected with that of the anarchy ruling – if one may use the phrase – throughout the forces of law and order in Algeria. He argued that if police officers who had taken to 'bad habits' were transferred to France, if the authority of the State was re-established in Algeria, if the Governor-General became in fact the commander instead of the pliable instrument of his staff, then the problem of violence would no longer exist. A remodelled police force could win the day and win it honourably. It was in fact M. Mendès-France's programme which M. Mairey made his own. We shall see later that it was also, *mutatis mutandis*, the programme of General de Gaulle.

Algeria was indeed 'under-administered', as Soustelle rightly emphasized. The apparatus of the French State really only spread out into the countryside through police officers of doubtful quality, and corrupt Muslims. But would it be possible to fill this administrative vacuum and to continue repression by more humane methods while still carrying on the war? In a second report dated 13 December 1955 M. Mairey was distinctly more pessimistic. He stated that although the administrative reform of the police was proceeding according to plan, the practice of torture was still spreading. The evidence which he quoted came from reports sent to him by police inspectors seconded to Algeria from France. One of these contained the following striking passage:

It is quite clear, after three months in this country, that no one can remain ignorant of the fact that these methods [torture] are generally employed. Our colleagues in Algeria make no secret of it and it must be admitted that their arguments to some extent justify the illegal procedures employed. They belong to a community where in practice there exist only two social strata: the European who has all the privileges, and the Muslim Frenchman who makes up the mass of the labour force and has always been considered as an inferior being; the behaviour of the police is inevitably affected by the attitude of mind thus engendered, especially as the vast majority of them come from settler families.

In these circumstances, the arrival of police officers or interrogators from France could only lead the police further down the path of deception. M. Mairey himself quotes an example of this, particularly striking because although it dates from November 1954 it is an exact forerunner even in the minutest detail of the Audin affair – which of course was the work of the parachute troops. A student, Belkacem Zeddour, had been arrested at the beginning of the insurrection as a Nationalist sympathizer and had not reappeared. Had he been a Muslim of poor family, probably no attempt to conceal the truth would have been made in his case; but his father, who was a rich merchant in Oran with many European friends, laid a complaint and an inquiry was opened. The police stated that Zeddour had escaped and had fled to Morocco. But, at the same time, certain highly placed persons in Algeria and some other police officers let it leak out that Zeddour had in fact died under the water torture in the police quarters in Algiers, and that after a fake escape his body

37

had been thrown into the sea off Cape Matifou. However, the lead with which his body had been weighted had been badly fixed and the body had been thrown up by the sea on 30 November 1954. It had been falsely identified by carefully schooled witnesses and buried in the European Cemetery. M. Mairey left behind him vigorous instructions that this affair should be cleared up. It never was.

Although by now he had few illusions, M. Mairey concluded his second report with a proposal stemming directly from the conclusions of his first. Two hundred commissioners and inspectors from the local police force should be sent back to France and replaced by a similar number from French Metropolitan territory. His advice was ignored, for it was already out of date. M. Mairey himself noted that already the police were not alone in using torture.

The police has had its part in these scandals but so has the Army. As responsible Head of the National Police Force, it is intolerable for me to think that, by their behaviour, French police officers can remind one of the Gestapo. Similarly as a Reserve Officer, I shudder when I hear French soldiers compared to the S.S. brutes of the Wehrmacht.

From 1954 to 1962, the police in Algeria used torture but the Army of the French Republic soon began to take up the running.

CHAPTER 3

Torture and the Army:
The Growth of the Power of the Military

IT is hard to say just when the police gave place to the military as the main organ of repression. For a long time the Government believed that it was dealing with a mere tribal rising requiring no more than police measures. But words can be useful tools of hypocrisy. After all, the war in Indo-China had throughout been termed a mere 'police operation'. In Algeria this expression seems to have been taken literally in that, although the realities of the law were almost continuously disregarded, certain legal form-alities were observed. M. Soustelle tells a story which there is no reason to disbelieve. At the beginning of the insurrection when a *fellegh* [rebel] was killed, the Public Prosecutor immediately opened an inquiry as he would have in the case of a murder in peacetime and the examining Magistrate would compel astonished, and often indignant, officers and soldiers to appear and justify their conduct in the face of the enemy, just as if they had committed a civil crime.*

However, on 20 August 1955 it was necessary to face facts. While the Moroccans were celebrating the second anniversary of the fall of the Sultan, Sidi Mohammed Ben Youssef, the Algerian insurgents suddenly came out into the open throughout the Department of Constantine. More than a hundred Europeans were massacred in Philippeville. In revenge the parachute troops executed on the spot more than 1,000 suspects, or supposed suspects. Full civil and military powers to put down the revolt in Philippeville were given to the Commander of a parachute unit, Colonel Château-Jobert (today one of the leaders of the O.A.S.). Whole settlements were destroyed and men, women, and children were massacred.

The war immediately took a new turn. On 22 August 1955,

* *Aimée et souffrante Algérie*, Paris, 1956.

the Government of M. Faure decided to recall some of the Reservists who had served towards the end of 1952. Less than a year later, in April 1956, the Government of M. Guy Mollet recalled all of them. There were less than 60,000 men in Algeria on 1 November 1954, but after that date the number rose to 500,000, not counting the European and Muslim auxiliary forces.

At this point the whole nature of the problem of torture underwent a fundamental change; it ceased to be a question of what was done by a few police officers or a minority of particularly brutal army officers. The entire youth of the French nation was brought face to face with the problem. Of course, not all the million-odd young Frenchmen who served in Algeria took part in torture sessions. Such a suggestion has never been made and it would be absurd if it were. Those in power (in particular M. Mollet) made a show of believing that this sort of accusation was being bandied about so that they could have an easy case to answer. But it is clear that from this period on the practice of torture became so general that it constituted a problem for the whole mass of young Frenchmen called up for service in Algeria. Still more important, the type of war being waged in Algeria could not be carried on at all without the simultaneous use *both of torture and of the mass of young conscripts drawn from the mother country*.

For the war waged by the F.L.N. was, by its very nature, a revolutionary war. Certainly this was true of the fighting techniques used, though perhaps less so of the economic and sociological objectives of the leaders of the insurrection, which in any case were somewhat nebulous at first. The stake in such a war, as the French experts on subversive warfare rightly perceived, is the conquest of the minds of the population. The main object of the insurrection was to bring about a state of affairs in which every Algerian in every town, in every *mechta* (collection of peasant huts), in every village, should be convinced that the cause of the F.L.N. was his own. Brutal methods were, if necessary, used to achieve this; those who collaborated with the French Army were executed and those who did not obey orders were punished. By the second half of 1956 this object had nearly been achieved. The old parties and the rival movement of Messali

Hadj had been, to all intents and purposes, eliminated. The A.L.N. (Armée de Libération Nationale – National Liberation Army), with its military units scouring the countryside and its terrorist networks, was only one, although the best-known, of the means employed in this revolutionary war. Contact with the population, and in particular with the peasant population, was maintained through the O.P.A. (Organisation Politico-administrative – Political and Administrative Organization) which knit together the revolutionary leaders in each village, each settlement, and each town. A reservist who served in Algeria, and who gave a particularly clear account of his experiences, painted the following picture of the O.P.A.:

It is responsible for propaganda, for collecting funds, for getting information, for supply, for the billeting and the provision of guides for A.L.N. units passing through. The O.P.A is at once a local armed militia, the political movement responsible for indoctrinating the masses in Algeria, and 'the fifth column' within the French Army. In Algeria, the group of children playing near by, the women fetching water from the well, the much-travelled and well-informed merchant, the *harki* [Auxiliary] in whom you have complete confidence, may all be O.P.A. members. Everywhere the O.P.A. has its informers and its spies whose task is to report to their leader the slightest piece of information of any interest regarding the movements of the Army of occupation. The O.P.A works everywhere in close cooperation with the A.L.N., and it maintains caches of arms, together with stocks of food and ammunition, in caves, tunnels, and other hiding places.*

In these circumstances the insurrection in Algeria was clearly developing into an Intelligence war in the military sense of the term, for it was being waged against a closely regimented population – and in such a situation torture tends to become a major weapon. Out in the country, although a commander may know from air reconnaissance where the enemy is operating, this knowledge is of little use if he does not know where that enemy draws his supplies and where his hideouts are. The same applies to the towns. Terrorist networks cannot be wiped out by killing or capturing front-line operators (who are in any case expendable);

* Michel Biran, *Deuxième classe en Algérie*, published by *Perspectives socialistes*, November 1961.

it is the real leaders, those who control the stocks of arms and bombs, who must be reached. The war in Algeria was therefore, in essence, a struggle against the O.P.A. In every town, every settlement, every village, the rebel organization had to be destroyed and the population brought under the closest possible control. The old police organization, as it existed at the outbreak of the insurrection, was totally inadequate for such a task. It could no longer count on controlling the population through the old Muslim headmen. The chess-board organization of the O.P.A. had to be matched by a similar military organization and this was why so large a force, necessarily composed primarily of young conscripts, was required. Not all of them, or even nearly all of them, saw active service. Comparatively few soldiers actually fought in Algeria; but they all contributed to the task of clamping the Algerian people in a strait-jacket and this took over seven years. They all played their part in the military victory to which General de Gaulle has so often referred. But the means of achieving that military victory inevitably involved political defeat.*

The methods of the F.L.N. led some of the officers responsible for military operations, and particularly officers of the parachute units, to work out a theory of revolutionary warfare. Many of them had served in Indo-China and so had already had experience of subversive war. They had read some of Mao Tse-tung's work and had learnt from them that a guerrilla organization must permeate the population 'like fish in water'. Although these theories were wrongly applied in practice and were ridiculed in France as brain children of intellectually mediocre colonels, they were nevertheless the product of profound and serious thought.

The clearest explanation of the essential features of the theory behind the French technique is to be found in a series of articles, lectures, and official memoranda by Colonel Argoud, who commanded a sector in Algeria from 1957 to 1960 and was then Chief-of-Staff of the Algiers Army Corps. (In 1961 he became one of the founders of the O.A.S.) Antoine Argoud summarized his

* The present political crisis in Algeria owes a great deal to the fact that, in destroying the O.P.A., the French Army killed so many of the best-educated and politically most sophisticated Algerians.

theory into the trinity of 'protection-commitment-supervision'.

What does this mean? In order to protect the population, the first essential step was to eliminate the 'foreign body', by which the military meant the rebel organization. This was impossible through the established legal procedures. Argoud made this quite clear on 21 December 1960, at a session *in camera* of the 'barricades' trial. He said:

'I was commanding the Arba sector during the battle of Algiers in 1957; although I had full legal powers I did not wish to have recourse to them because I was responsible for the lives both of the troops and civilians; so, after an exhaustive and detailed inquiry carried out with the assistance of Inspectors of the criminal police, I gave orders that those who had committed murder or were leaders of the insurrection should be publicly executed by a firing-squad in the square.'

Such actions were to become frequent. Argoud himself has said that in a small village in Algeria, the O.P.A. organization reformed ten times in three years, despite public executions having been carried out in the village square. Because it was the O.P.A. that constituted the link between the population and the rebellion, it was only by the elimination of the O.P.A. that the Muslims could be reduced to that docile, pliable mass of humanity considered by the army to be an essential condition of success.

In order to 'protect' and to administer the population, it was necessary to 're-group' it. Even 500,000 men could not be everywhere at once in the enormous territory of Algeria. The nomadic tribes therefore had to be concentrated, the mountain tribes brought down into the plain, and both located in easily accessible areas, later to be surrounded by barbed wire. That these areas looked like concentration camps, or that those 'regrouped' driven from their lands and pastures might well die of hunger, worried nobody.

Once the population was 'protected' the next step was to produce 'commitments', in other words a proportion of the Muslim population had to be forced to collaborate with the forces of oppression. Attempts were made, if necessary by force, and by promises of security and good pay, to recruit auxiliaries, *harkis,* among prisoners taken from the maquis. The intention was to use these auxiliaries to set up a counter-guerrilla organization; but of course the auxiliaries were also available for more despicable jobs (in the same way as the Germans had frequently used the French Milice, the special auxiliary police force raised by the Vichy government, during the war) so that the officers could keep their hands clean.

A note from Corps Headquarters, Algiers, drafted by Colonel Argoud, laid down the following:

The necessary systematic search for mines in an area or on a section of road should be entrusted to a number of heads of families, who should be given a reward for each mine found. The heads of families chosen should be those anxious for money and those who have a large number of dependants, i.e. children, relatives, friends, protégés, shepherds, etc. It is the latter who actually do the searching.

Finally more official and semi-official police were needed to control the population. Police officers in charge of rural or urban areas were enjoined to keep a permanent card-index recording the attitude of everybody in their territory. An official instruction from the headquarters of a colonial infantry regiment, clearly inspired by Colonel Argoud's teaching, gives the following examples of the sort of daily notes which the officer in charge should make in his diary, or 'contacts book';

A group of women were picking olives at such and such a place; one of them seemed to be on the watch.
For the second day in succession Mrs Z. put a white sheet out to dry beside her hut.
I have the impression that the attitude of the children towards the troops is less friendly than it was a few days ago.

Recalcitrants who would not accept supervision, or who tried to evade it, were, in Colonel Argoud's words, to be 'sent to the bottom of the wadi'.

This picture of an Algeria turned into a concentration camp totally under the control of the army was logic gone mad; it was not the ideal of every officer serving there. In his novel *La Grotte* published in 1961, Colonel Georges Buis is highly critical of this concept of pacification. The hero of his book tries to destroy the military power of the F.L.N. without affecting the distribution of the population or preventing it running its own affairs.

But there was a possibility that this less oppressive attitude might be no more than a pipe dream. Was it really possible to fight the A.L.N. without at the same time destroying the O.P.A.? Whatever the theoretical arguments, the fact remains that a large number of officers, particularly those in the S.A.S. (Sections Administratives Spécialisées – Special Administrative Sections),* felt that the right way to conduct the war was by looking after the population, constructing schools, and setting up hospitals. They at least had a clear conscience. But a group of young soldiers put their fingers on the essence of the problem when they wrote, in perhaps unnecessarily harsh terms:

. . .the soldier turned schoolmaster, the S.A.S. officer, even the doctor of the Free Medical Service are not just teachers, administrators, and doctors; they are military personnel and are never allowed to forget it. In this war, which is overturning all our values, they are not primarily serving the Muslim children, or the sick of the village; they are serving a cause; they are one more weapon in the battle. The army only supports the S.A.S. system because it plays this dual role.†

There were cases in which an army or civilian doctor revived a wounded man merely in order that he might be tortured; but apart from such extreme cases it was perfectly possible for one officer, whose own standard of conduct might be irreproachable, to hand over a prisoner to another officer whose job it would be to torture or kill him; for a schoolmaster or social worker to be turned into a more or less conscious agent of propaganda for the most outrageous ideas. The very nature of this war meant that those who were merely conscientiously doing their duty were in fact working on behalf of the torturers.

From the moral point of view torture was the most significant facet of this totalitarian system, but it was only one facet among others which were perhaps more important historically or sociologically. And of course the whole system was not set up in a

* The S.A.S., set up by M. Soustelle in 1955, were centres of local administration in country areas run by officers who were initially recruited from ex-officers of the Native Affairs Service in Morocco.

† 'La Pacification', eye-witness account by a group of young conscripts, *Esprit*, January 1961.

day. Indeed it was never perfected, for the army was eventually forced to leave Algeria after the Évian agreements, and as soon as the cease fire was signed, the F.L.N., through the O.P.A., once more became masters of the countryside; particularly in the provinces of Constantine and Algiers, where the Algerians were able to reform their organization whenever it was destroyed.

Some conscripts, and indeed some members of the regular army, were opposed to the role which authority wished them to play. Some sections in the civil administration conducted a rear-guard action, which was not entirely without its effects. But in spite of all this Algeria was gradually taken over by an autonomous military authority, the spear-head of which was formed by the teams of torturers who step by step ousted the representatives of established authority.

Obviously this situation was not reached in one full swoop. The first available accounts of the military machine of oppression are those from the earlier conscript classes; according to Professor Laurent Schwartz they give 'a terrible impression of horror and disorder'; in all or almost all areas where actual fighting was taking place, the Aurès and the Kabylie for example, torture and the murder of prisoners became normal practice. Certain units and certain personnel became 'specialists' in these horrors; examples were the parachute troops and the 'mobile rural police squads', who were in general recruited from among the Europeans of Algeria. But we must not over-generalize. Some commanders such as Colonel (later General) Pâris de Bollardière refused to use torture; some preferred to liquidate their prisoners immediately; others took evasive action, restraining their troops, who were in general only too eager to take reprisals, but doing so only in order to be able to hand their prisoners over to police officers or 'intelligence officers' who were expert at 'exploiting' their victims, in using torture to extract valuable information. In so far as the higher command had any say, it tended to favour this latter procedure rather than the straight murder of prisoners.

In the country areas the authority of the civil government had never been very firmly established, and it now gradually gave way to the authority of the Army. In 1956 three military commanders in country areas were vested with full powers; in Aurès there was General Parlange, actually given his authority by M. Soustelle as early as 1955, assisted by General Vanuxem (now in prison as a leader of the O.A.S. in France); in Kabylie there was General Olié; and in the Blida Atlas Colonel de Bollardière. The use to which this authority was put was obviously not the same in each case and it was a cruel turn of fate that it should have been Argoud who commanded the sector adjoining that of de Bollardière and who ultimately took over from him. So out in the country the civil power abdicated and its place was taken by a military authority, one of whose weapons was torture.

In the large cities and their immediate vicinity, matters did not develop so quickly. Although the specialist torturers, whose activities had been brought to light by the Wuillaume Report, continued to carry on their trade in Algiers, Oran, and Constantine, the large towns were, during 1955 and the first half of 1956, havens of peace compared to the country areas. The civil administration continued to exercise some measure of control. The internment camps for suspects, which the administration organized by virtue of its special powers,* were not modelled on Nazi concentration camps, and those who were detained in them were at least assured that they would not be tortured.

It was however in Algiers that dramatic and decisive events took place which eventually led to the extension throughout Algeria of the military power which already ruled in the countryside. On 6 February 1956 the Prime Minister, M. Mollet, was received in Algiers with a shower of rotten eggs and tomatoes; he immediately threw up the sponge, demanded the resignation of General Catroux as Governor-General, and replaced him by M. Robert Lacoste. The Army played no part in this disturbance, though some of the police, particularly police officers who had been involved in torturing and were afraid of being transferred to Metropolitan France, connived at it. They had no cause for anxiety. A few high officials, notably the Director of the Sûreté in Algeria, were replaced, but on the whole the police organization remained intact. We have already seen what the attitude of mind of the police was. They were now backed up by territorial

* See Chapter 4.

units (a sort of Home Guard) recruited from the European population and in some cases even provided with armoured vehicles.

In a few weeks, between June and August 1956, a tragic situation suddenly developed. On 19 June the first guillotining of two
members of the F.L.N. took place in the Barbarossa Prison
courtyard. On 20 June, the F.L.N. replied by organizing the first
random attacks against the European population. The Europeans thereupon set up counter-terrorist cells and in the words
of one of them, Philippe Castille (now in prison as the leader of
the plastic bombers in the Paris area) 'raised counter-terrorism
from a mere craft to an industry'. One group under Castille and
Michel Fechoz bombed out a whole block of flats in the Casbah
during the night of 10–11 August 1956. There were several dozen
dead. Michel Fechoz and Philippe Castille could afford to boast
openly that they were the perpetrators of this crime; no action
was taken against them and the Press merely announced that a
secret F.L.N. arsenal had blown up. It is interesting to note that
this was the first indiscriminate plastic bomb attack in Algiers
and that it was the work of Frenchmen. The F.L.N. replied by
organizing bomb attacks in its turn; these exchanges were the
forerunners of the battle of Algiers.

By the end of 1956 it was clear that the situation in Algiers
was similar to that in the countryside, and the question of
authority therefore became urgent. The extremists in Algiers
had been thinking this problem over for some time, and had
realized that no movement had any chance of doing more than
simple counter-terrorism unless it could link itself to the army.
General Faure, Deputy Commander of the Algiers area and
organizer of the territorial armoured units, thereupon got in
touch with certain extremist circles in Paris and with some
counter-terrorist groups who already had a number of attacks
to their credit. Some of these, in particular the C.R.F. (Comité
de la Renaissance Française – Committee for the Revival of
French Authority) run by Robert Martel and R. Vinciguerra
(now Deputy for Algiers) had organized *private* torture chambers
where they carried out 'interrogations' with the agreement of a
number of officers, particularly Colonel Thomazo. General
Faure worked out a plan to seize power, but he was naïve enough

to think that M. Paul Teitgen, Secretary-General in overall charge of the police in the prefecture of Algiers, might join the conspiracy, and so Faure disclosed the plan to him on 24 December 1956, whereupon Teitgen immediately denounced it.

It was not however the end of this conspiracy, for such punishments as were inflicted were insignificant; General Faure, for instance, was merely sentenced to thirty days house arrest. So counter-terrorist exploits continued. On 29 December, during the funeral of M. Froger, President of the Association of Mayors of the Algiers department, who had been murdered in somewhat doubtful circumstances, there was a demonstration during which the cry of 'Put the army in charge' was heard for the first time, and the Europeans then ran amok.

There was no lack of officers ready to respond to this invitation. They were still brooding over their political defeat at Suez and their amazement at the lack of results from the hi-jacking of Ben Bella's aeroplane on 22 October 1956. Moreover, like the rest of the European population, they were uneasy at the offensive spirit shown by the F.L.N., now calling for a general strike at the end of January. Everything indicated that they were unlikely to get the better of the insurrection and terrorism in the towns by traditional methods, still less by legal procedure.

It was at precisely this moment, during those last decisive days of 1956, that M. Mairey arrived in Algeria on his second visit which lasted from 15 to 18 December. He was constantly followed, not only by his own staff but by members of the staffs of M. Lacoste and the Prefect of Algiers, which further complicated his position. In the report which he submitted to the Government on 2 January 1957, M. Mairey no longer confined himself to technical questions; he no longer felt that the solution lay merely in a reform of the police; and he took issue with the official line, which he summarized in these words:

The vital military objectives have been attained, but as a result terrorism has withdrawn into the towns. Although this makes terrorism more difficult to combat, it is not at the moment an exceptionally serious problem.

M. Mairey easily proved that deception was more than ever the order of the day in Algeria, and that a number of military commanders were lending their authority to the vilest atrocities, such as the massacre of Muslims at Medea on 15 December 1956 when police dogs were let loose on those who had not been crushed by armoured cars. M. Mairey ended his report.

To any who may still be labouring under the illusion that the problem of Algeria can still be solved by force, i.e. the combined force of the army and the police, I reply that that is a dangerous day-dream because from now on it cannot be done. After so much violence and injustice the gap is too wide, the hatred too acute, the lack of understanding too complete, for Algeria to become a real entity once more, except as a result of some major upheaval.*

On 7 January 1957, M. Serge Baret, the Senior Prefect of Algiers, acting on the orders of M. Lacoste, signed a decree delegating police powers in the Department of Algiers to General Massu, Commander of the 10th Parachute Division. As a result the responsibility for liquidating terrorism in the city, and breaking the general strike called for by the F.L.N., fell not to any civil authority but to General Massu. So now the Army was legally and officially in power. Algeria had come to the parting of the ways, and the road taken led straight to the unconditional surrender of the civil power to the military, in other words of the French Republic to the 'Generals'.

I do not propose to give an account of the 'Battle of Algiers', the name used to describe the action of the 10th Parachute Division, which culminated at the end of September with Ali La Pointe, the last terrorist leader still at liberty, blowing himself up with his last explosives in his hide-out in the Casbah. It is already well known that in the battle of Algiers torture was systematically used as a weapon. General Massu came out firmly in support of these methods. Father Delarue, the chaplain of the 10th Parachute Division, set at rest any religious scruples the General might have had by drafting a note, with the help of Colonel Trinquier, in which torture was compared to the slap which a father gives a disobedient child or to a painful but neces-

* After this report M. Mairey was forbidden entry into Algeria, though later, on 19 August 1957, he was recalled by M. Bourgès-Maunoury.

sary surgical operation. In another note published by the French *Students' Review* in Algiers, Father Delarue wrote:

Faced with a choice between two evils, either to cause temporary suffering to a bandit taken in the act who in any case deserves to die, or to leave numbers of innocent people to be massacred by this criminal's gang, when it could be destroyed as a result of his information, there can be no hesitation in choosing the lesser of the two evils, in an effective but not sadistic interrogation.

General Massu, who had had himself subjected to the electrical torture in order the better to be able to judge its effects, was delighted with this pronouncement; in a note dated 19 March 1957 which bore two somewhat contradictory headings 'Secret' and for 'General Distribution throughout Z.N.A.' (Northern Zone of the department of Algiers) he wrote:

A *sine qua non* of our action in Algeria is that we should accept these methods heart and soul as necessary and morally justifiable.

The essential lesson which emerges from the battle of Algiers is clear; to study its course is to see the birth of a totalitarian system. True, there was some resistance, for instance from certain civil government circles headed by the Secretary-General in charge of police in the Algiers prefecture, M. Teitgen, and the senior police official of Algiers, M. Jean Builles who, though Algerian born, was a convinced Republican. But these brave men had no one to work with; all they could do was to keep themselves informed and in turn keep their superiors informed. (It was M. Teitgen and M. Builles who passed on the information that Maurice Audin, Assistant Professor of Science at Algiers University and a member of the Algerian Communist Party, had been strangled by Lieutenant Charbonnier* of the Parachute Division, although he was said to have escaped on 21 June 1957.) Just one string of power did remain in their hands however, for they were still the only people authorized to sign 'confinement orders', which, in the absence of a legal decision, were the only means of regularizing arrests made by the military. M. Paul

---

* The essential facts of this affair were published in English by Peter Benenson in the first chapter of *Persecution 1961*, Penguin Books, Harmondsworth, 1961.

Teitgen was compelled to sign no fewer than 24,000 confinement orders and he has himself stated that of this number 3,024 persons disappeared having either died under torture or been summarily executed. These figures, whose sole merit is that they are official, undoubtedly do not give the full picture. The military authorities did not disclose all the arrests they made. Moreover in June 1957 they managed to lay hands on the census documents, and were thus able to wipe out all trace, other than in the memory of the family concerned, of anyone who had been arrested and killed. M. Teitgen could count the number of persons who had disappeared and he could make reports; but he could not stop the torture and massacre. On 12 September 1957 he drew the only logical conclusion from his failure and resigned. Civil authority had had its day in Algeria; only military authority remained. This we shall now try to describe.

The parachute troops swept through the city and things began to move quickly. By 8 January in the Algiers area alone 950 'confinement orders' had been issued. On 4 February in a note to M. Lacoste, General Salan, the Commander-in-Chief, wrote: 'In so far as we can see at present, we must expect to have up to 20,000 people on our hands by the middle of March.' On 23 July, reporting on the Algiers area, General Massu wrote to his immediate superior, General Allard:

In my view the only solution lies in setting up a camp capable of holding at least ten thousand. This would involve the disbandment of three or four of the smaller camps. The cost of this would be more than outweighed by the resulting economies in guard personnel. The possibility of locating this camp on an island should be considered.

While awaiting this development, the Algiers Area Headquarters opened its own concentration camp, Paul-Cazelles, on 6 February 1957, and detailed as guard unit the Foreign Legion Parachute Regiment (the Green Berets). The confusion was such (this was stated officially) that many of those present did not appear on the lists, while the same lists included many who were not present but had either escaped or become victims of 'work in the woods' (slang for summary execution). If there was an 'accident' *en route*, random arrests were made to fill the vacant places. The ill-treatment meted out in this camp became such a scandal that eventually a military unit at Orléansville published an indictment more damning than any of the many accusations made by its inmates.

The city of Algiers itself was divided into eight sub-sectors, each of which had its own 'sorting centre' which included a torture chamber. Villa Susini, run by the 1st Foreign Legion Parachute Regiment, was one such sorting centre; the El-Biar block of flats, where Henri Alleg was tortured and Maurice Audin assassinated, was another. Above these there were two major sorting centres, Beni-Messous and Ben-Aknoun, which were the only centres officially known to the civil administration. We must not, however, be misled into thinking that there was any real organization; in fact there was none. The colonels commanding sub-sectors were little more than administrators who simply lent their quarters to the men of the 10th Parachute Division. Thus the colonel commanding Fort Emperor barracks could write with a perfectly clear conscience to the wife of a man who had disappeared after having been tortured in some military establishment in his sub-sector:

Although I am in command of Fort Emperor barracks I have no knowledge of the fate of those persons who have been quartered here. I have never been responsible for any act of repression. My quarters have simply been put at the disposal of those responsible for the maintenance of order.

It was at Fort Emperor that Maurice Audin was secretly buried after he had been murdered by Lieutenant Charbonnier.

The real work of repression was in fact not carried out at sub-sector level but at the headquarters of the sector Algiers-Sahel, commanded from 10 June 1957 onwards by Colonel Godard, who was the true master of Algiers. A 'brains trust', to use General Massu's expression, under Lieutenant-Colonel Trinquier, head of the 'offensive Intelligence' section, collected information and took the important decisions. (Trinquier later emerged as a real specialist in repression and torture, for which he expounded a theory in a book entitled *La Guerre moderne*.) He had under his orders a team of Intelligence officers who were distributed throughout the various sub-sectors. These were the real masters and they constituted a complete clandestine organization; at El-Biar, for instance, Lieutenant Charbonnier used two rooms which had as it were 'extra-territorial status'; even the police had no right to enter them. The police itself worked in double harness with the Intelligence officers of the sub-sector: Captain Devis and Lieutenant Erulin, whom Henri Alleg described in *La Question*. A specialist in torture, Captain Faulques, who recently reappeared as one of the organizers of Mr Tshombe's army, was the contact man between the various Intelligence officers under Colonel Trinquier and gave them technical assistance where necessary; Captain de la Bourdonnaye-Montluc, also later a Katanga mercenary, was the personal representative of Colonel Godard in this organization, Major Aussaresses was responsible for liaison with the criminal police, and Major Le Mire was General Massu's personal representative. To judge from their various duties there can be no doubt that *every one* of these men must have been personally involved in any affair as serious as that of Audin and thus involved in the scandal raised by the murder of this young Algiers mathematics professor.

The set-up outlined above was at first purely empirical. Gradually however it took shape and acquired a name. In July 1957 the organization took on the dual title of C.C.I. (Centre de Co-ordination Interarmées – Inter-service Coordination Centre), to show that it included representatives of all three services, and D.O.P. (Dispositif Opérationel de Protection – Operational Security Organization). Under this name of C.C.I./D.O.P. the organization continued in existence after the battle of Algiers and even after the 10th Parachute Division had left the city. We shall shortly see what was its role.*

But an efficiently organized machine was not enough; it would have been working in a vacuum if it had not been supported by local personnel recruited from both the European and Muslim populations. On 4 March 1957 M. Lacoste's staff announced the setting up in Algiers of a Dispositif de Protection Urbaine (D.P.U. – Urban Security Service). (It had initially been named 'Groupes de Protection Urbaine' (G.P.U. – Urban

* See Chapter 4.

Security Groups) but its creators had recoiled before these initials.) It was in fact a supplementary police force composed of Europeans and intended to regiment the city. There was no need to supervise the inhabitants of the European areas: it was the Muslims who worked there who were subject to constant surveillance. Thus one of the initial demands of the extremists was met and counter-terrorism became an integral part of the official apparatus of repression.

When the Algiers-Sahel staff submitted the list of the leaders of the D.P.U. to the civil authorities, they noted with astonishment that among them was Dr Kovacs, who had been arrested at the end of January for his part in the bazooka attack of 16 January against General Salan (suspected at the time of blacklegging) and who had been an active participant in a private torture chamber set up in the Villa des Sources in the suburbs of Algiers.

From March on each block and each house in the European quarter had its D.P.U. leader. The Muslims of the Casbah were supervised and regimented by ex-rebels who were responsible with their lives for what went on in each house and who, from their uniform, were dubbed 'Blue Caps'. Colonel Trinquier had succeeded in proving that torture was 'something which could be organized'.

Since the real specialists among the parachute troops were fully employed in Algiers, the organization was weaker in the Oran and Constantine departments where the Algiers solution was not used until later. However, these areas were not without able organizers. In Constantine, the prefect was M. Maurice Papon, later renowned for his repression of both Algerians and democratically minded Frenchmen, while the prefect at Oran was M. Lambert, who had not hesitated to justify the use of torture when giving evidence before the 'international commission for the suppression of concentration camps'.

Sorting centres similar to those in Algiers were in operation everywhere. In some areas indeed the integration of the police into the army was carried further than in Algiers, where M. Teitgen had raised desperate opposition to it. In an official circular dated 11 April 1957, M. Lacoste wrote:

I draw your attention to the importance of organizing combined inter-rogation centres where the army can work together with the various police forces; the object of these is to speed up preliminary and semi-official inquiries. Such centres are already operating at Orléansville and Constantine. They appear to be completely satisfactory.

The Orléansville centre, which was set up in an old barn, and the Constantine centre, which was in Améziane Farm, turned into real conveyor-belt establishments where torture was applied with scientific precision. There were even training schools for this 'science'. At Philippeville Colonel Bigeard set up a 'training centre for subversive warfare' in May 1958, where the rules of torture proposed for the police by Inspector-General Wuillaume were taught.

Nevertheless this system had its gaps and its set backs. Some officers hung back. In the March 1957 number of the confiden-tial bulletin *Message des forces armées* the following appeared:

The struggle against the F.L.N. cells has meant that officers all too often have to do a police job. Official directives may indeed have kept silent on this subject, but it is hypocritical to try and deny that this situation exists or to minimize the serious effects upon the morale of the officers concerned. Turning officers into experts in third-degree police methods, into prosecutors, into high-level executioners, gives rise to a most serious problem. Although some are prepared to accept this state of affairs as a necessary evil, the best officers are disgusted by a degrading job which achieves nothing.

One officer went even further. In a directive dated 16 February 1957 General Massu called for 'increased policing effort'. General de Bollardière, General Massu's subordinate in command of the Blida Atlas, drafted a directive dated 18 February to implement this policy. In this directive he 'interpreted' General Massu's circular as follows: 'We must not be tempted, like some totali-tarian countries, to regard certain methods of obtaining informa-tion as normal procedure; these procedures are explicitly forbidden.' General Massu took exception to this 'interpretation'; General Salan and his civil superiors backed him up and General de Bollardière asked to be relieved of his command.

When General Massu was in command in Algiers, the most junior corporal in the Parachute Regiment had full police powers.

In the countryside, mere junior officers had to all intents and purposes power of life and death over a vast population. Such a situation was bound to raise the whole problem of the authority of the State, for this was both practically and morally the true point at issue.

From all practical points of view, the civil power in Algiers had literally vanished. After the resignation of M. Teitgen, the Army took over control of the Compagnies Républicaines de Sécurité (C.R.S. – Republican Security Companies), the sole remaining police force available for such jobs as sealing off a road in front of a demonstration, such as the one which occurred on 6 February. The Prefect of Algiers, M. Baret, to whom in theory General Massu was subordinate, became a mere agent of the military authorities. No civil authority could give an order to the police without permission from the colonel commanding the Algiers-Sahel Sector, i.e. Colonel Godard. Furthermore, through the D.P.U. and the Territorial Units, the Army could in a few hours mobilize large numbers of armed civilians, and, through the blue caps, they could at any moment produce on the 'forum' in front of the Central Government Building, a crowd of terrorized Muslims under threat that if they did not do what they were told they would be deprived of their identity cards, without which they would be outlaws and could be arrested or beaten like stray dogs.

The military torturers, although they held a terrifying degree of power, were, nevertheless, theoretically unprotected by the law. Cases occurred in which they were summoned as witnesses before a military examining magistrate or even, as in the case of the Audin affair, before a civil judge. In France, their names gradually became known in spite of, or perhaps because of, seizures of newspapers. Moreover, neither the military torturers nor the generals under whose authority they worked, had by 1957 achieved a state of mind comparable to that of the S.S., in which crime was calmly accepted provided it was committed in accordance with orders, though many of them were to arrive at that later. If one reads what some of these men have written to justify themselves, what is particularly surprising is their attempt to justify the use of torture without having the courage to use the actual word. Even General Massu, unlike Inspector-General Wuillaume, never actually speaks of torture or of using water or electricity. He speaks of 'clandestine and counter-revolutionary methods' and yet he is one of the most outspoken of the Generals. Others, though they back up their subordinates, do not put things as clearly. For instance, during the night of 14–15 March 1957, Lieutenant Curutchet of the 7th Infantry Regiment incarcerated 101 suspects in wine-cellars at Ain Isser in the Department of Oran. The next day forty-one were dead from suffocation. Lieutenant Curutchet was charged but never sentenced; his superior commanders backed him up. General Pedron, the Corps Commander at Oran, did no more than refer to 'regrettable incidents' and send out a circular on 'sanitation in quarters'.* Lieutenant Curutchet is now a deserter and a leader of the O.A.S.

These men were therefore bound together, accomplices in nameless horrors. They thus became true 'conspirators' in the etymological sense of the word, for they had breathed the same fetid air. An officer once assured the writer Jules Roy, who was himself a retired air force colonel and Algerian-born:

If the hearing of the Audin case comes off, I know officers who have already *sworn on the Bible* not to tell the truth and who will never tell it because they are convinced heart and soul that the truth would render a disservice to their country.

So bonds of conspiracy were formed between the specialist operators in the 'sorting centres', the counter-terrorist craftsmen and the members of the different gangs both in Paris and in Algiers who were plotting the downfall of the régime; all became inextricably linked. These men realized that 'there was no need to seize power; it merely needed picking up', to quote a phrase attributed to General de Gaulle. Should a Government willing to negotiate come to power in Paris and so challenge the authority of the military in Algeria, there were now men ready to take time by the forelock and sweep away the last vestiges of civilian power.

This is exactly what was to happen one evening in May 1958.

* These facts are set out in a report by M. Delavignette, a member of the Safeguards Commission set up in April 1957 by the Mollet Government.

M. Pflimlin presented himself as Prime Minister to the National Assembly on 13 May. He was considered to be a firm advocate of negotiation; this was largely untrue but it was enough. The D.P.U. mobilized. A number of paratroopers in mufti from the Godard and Trinquier organizations and a number of students under the leadership of a young lawyer, Pierre Lagaillarde, an ex-paratrooper and an ex-torturer of the Villa Susini, appeared before the Central Government Building, which was guarded by the C.R.S. The Staff withdrew the C.R.S. and replaced them by parachute troops of the R.P.C. (the Colonial Parachute Regiment commanded by Colonel Trinquier). The Central Government building was accordingly 'taken' without difficulty. The torturers did not 'seize power', they merely proved that they had it already. It is doubtful whether such an enterprise would have been possible had not a similar story been unfolding in France itself among the leaders of the Republic. This story ran parallel to, and was to some extent the logical consequence of, the story of Algiers. The methods used were perhaps different, but the outcome was the same: the disappearance of the Republican form of State. It is to this story that we now turn.

CHAPTER 4

The Period of Lies

'FRANCE' – that was the operative word. A priest of the 'French Mission', Robert Davèzies, used to try to find out what the children in Algeria were thinking and accounts of his talks with them were published in *Le Front*.* He found that these children did not usually say, 'The French Army committed such and such a crime or Lieutenant so-and-so tortured my father,' they said simply, 'France.' But who represents France? – presumably the officers who reached positions of power in Algeria as a result of a long process of conquest based upon the systematic use of torture; presumably also the 'French of Algeria' who were responsible for the events of May 1958; but primarily the Prime Ministers, Ministers, and Members of the Assembly, who speak in the name of the country, who keep the country informed, who lay down policy, and who put it into execution.

From 1 November 1954 to 1 June 1958, the France of Paris was represented successively by M. Pierre Mendès-France, M. Edgar Faure, M. Guy Mollet, M. Bourgès-Maunoury, M. Félix Gaillard, and M. Pierre Pflimlin. 'France in Algeria', as General de Gaulle subsequently called it, was represented by M. Roger Léonard until 1 February 1955, then by M. Jacques Soustelle until 9 February 1956 and by M. Robert Lacoste from then until 13 May 1958.

The following questions must now be answered: Had the military and police officers who used torture any right to do so? Had the leaders of the State, given either orally or in writing, any instruction which might tend to establish the systematic use of torture? Was it good enough for them simply to play the part of a Pontius Pilate? Had they made any attempt to stop or check the pitiless march of events before those events overtook them?

* Éditions de Minuit, 1959.

On 27 March 1957, M. Mollet, summing up a debate in the National Assembly, said:

'The Government, the Army, and the civil administration are accused of having had recourse to unmentionable procedures, even to systematic torture. The problem with which we are faced, therefore, is indeed one of the utmost gravity. To put it more clearly, the questions are these: Have there been licensed excesses, and if so were they in accordance with the policy of the Government, the Army, and the civil administration? Or have these excesses been forbidden, and if orders forbidding them have been issued, have the culprits been discovered and have they been punished? Finally, what has been done to anticipate and prevent similar situations in the future?'

These are exactly the questions which I too must now try to answer.

In Algeria it had become more or less a tradition that the Governor-General signed circulars forbidding the use of torture without taking much trouble to see that his orders were obeyed. M. Léonard certainly followed this tradition; but when an Algerian member of the Assembly, M. Benbhamed, lamented that the Governor-General was never obeyed, all that happened was that M. Max Lejeune, who was then a Socialist Opposition Member, cried, 'If he is not obeyed, then he is not a Governor.' We have already seen how M. Soustelle reacted when confronted with the facts reported by Inspector-General Wuillaume and the conclusions of his inquiry. After the events of 20 August 1955, however, M. Soustelle evidently considered that it was not enough merely to back up his subordinates. On 22 August he announced in an official public communiqué that ten settlements suspected of harbouring rebels had been completely destroyed; he added, however, that the women and children, though not the men, had been evacuated. This statement at least had the merit of being candid. Yet at the same time M. Soustelle was assuring M. Mairey of his complete support with his inquiry, even though that inquiry led him to demand punishment for those military and police officers who had used torture. In the large volume of memoirs of his period as Governor-General which M. Soustelle published on his return from Algeria he was quite prepared to pass over in complete silence all that he must, in his official position, have known about the torturing which had occurred; yet on 14 November 1955, in a 'letter on the subject of Algeria from one intellectual to another' M. Soustelle, referring to his own background, wrote:

Even when acting in an official capacity, at heart I was still a University Professor, a teacher, and a writer. I believe in the intrinsic value of thought, research, and reflection. I am convinced that we intellectuals have a part to play in public life, if only in attempting to substitute for the vague and emotional ideas which are the normal stuff of which politics are made, the ideal of unswerving devotion to truth and honesty which our profession teaches us.

But however eminent a personality a Governor-General in Algiers may have been, he was no more than a public servant. Divorced from Paris and isolated in the labyrinthine Government building in the Forum he tended quickly to become the servant, not of the Government in Paris, but of his own staff. The fact that those often thought to be most 'liberal' have turned 'tyrant' has been ascribed to the atmosphere of Algiers. M. Robert Lacoste who, after General Catroux's brief interregnum was M. Soustelle's successor, was actually a Minister in his own right in the Government of M. Mollet and in those of M. Bourgès-Maunoury and M. Gaillard. He thus carried greater responsibility than that normally borne by the Governor-General, and it was therefore more difficult for his government to disown him. Others who shared responsibility for Algeria with him were M. Bourgès-Maunoury, who was Minister of Defence in M. Mollet's Government and later Prime Minister and M. Lejeune. who was Secretary of State for the Armed Forces from 1 February 1956 to 13 May 1958.

There can be no doubt that M. Lacoste, the representative of France in Algeria, and with him M. Lejeune and M. Bourgès-Maunoury, gave their approval to the practice of torture. M. Lacoste quickly showed where he stood. When he received the special correspondent of *L'Express*, Patrick Kessel, on 16 February 1956, he shouted:

'You can report that we have not executed criminals although we have had them under lock and key. Some have already been condemned to death three times. We are the most patient country in the world, yet if I were to execute these creatures the intellectuals would label me a monster.'

And then, giving the accepted army view, he added, 'We have been waging war with the criminal code in our pockets.'*

The battle of Algiers led M. Lacoste to commit himself even further. When the quarrel between General de Bollardière and General Massu erupted he supported General Massu, and his colleagues in the Mollet Government agreed with him. On 24 March 1957, M. Teitgen tried to resign for the first time and on that occasion he wrote:

In the last three months, it has become clear to me that we have entered not merely upon a phase of disrespect for the law, which is of little importance in war, but upon a faceless phase in which no one is responsible; and this can only end in war crimes. I would never make a statement like this had I not, during recent visits to the internment camps of Paul-Cazelles and Beni-Messous, seen on certain of the inmates clear marks of the same cruelties and tortures which I myself suffered fourteen years ago in the Gestapo cellars in Nancy.

But Lacoste did no more than refuse his resignation and put a little order into the disorderly actions of the parachute troops.

M. Teitgen's views were supported by M. Reliquet, an ex-Public Prosecutor of Algiers; in a sworn statement made on 5 July 1960 before the Examining Magistrate of Rennes who was conducting the inquiry into the Audin case, he said:

In spite of the circumstantial reports published in the Press, in spite of certain approaches to the Government and to M. Robert Lacoste himself pointing out the serious dangers implied by these abuses, nothing was done either to repudiate the use of violence, to punish those responsible, or to forbid its continuation in the future; on the contrary (I have this from General Allard) certain Ministers, in particular MM. Lacoste, Bourgès-Maunoury, and Lejeune encouraged it.

M. Reliquet's statement was confirmed by General Allard on 4 October 1960:

I have been present personally during a number of visits made by MM. Bourgès-Maunoury, Lacoste, and Max Lejeune to a number of sector

* Patrick Kessel, 'The Civil Power, the Army and Torture', *Les Temps modernes*, August–September 1960.

headquarters and on each occasion, these authorities gave orders that the war should be pursued with the utmost possible vigour. I remember in particular a visit to the headquarters of Col. Bigeard during which he produced statistics to show that he had destroyed approximately three-quarters of the rebel organization in his sector. One of the Ministers present congratulated him and encouraged him to carry on and finish the job. I cannot now remember which Minister this was; I think it was M. Lejeune but I cannot be sure of this. I can, however, still see Colonel Bigeard replying 'Mr Minister, as you can well imagine, results such as these are not achieved by pussyfoot methods'. The only reply was that he should be careful that too much mud did not stick.

Officers like Colonel Bigeard probably hoped that M. Lacoste, M. Lejeune, and M. Bourgès-Maunoury would go further, and actually issue written instructions on the subject. But in his written instructions, M. Lacoste never did more than emphasize 'his complete confidence in the Army, in its dignified attitude in Algeria, in its patriotism, in its grasp of its great and noble task, in its efficiency, in its humanity, in its devotion and spirit of self-sacrifice'. Phrases such as these only increased what has been called the 'mental confusion of the Army'. Officers responsible for using torture were astounded to be summoned as witnesses by Judges when they thought that they had been fully covered by authority. Jean Lartéguy, an ex-officer of a parachute regiment, put their feelings well when he put these words into the mouth of a character in his novel who represents Colonel Bigeard:

Whenever ministers or deputies come to our headquarters, I say to them, 'That only happens on the side. We do it because the Government has ordered us to do it but it disgusts and sickens us.' Some pretend not to understand or think that I am just joking. Others reply with little gestures of approval, 'You are doing it for France', and now the same bastards want to try us for it.

We have already seen the extent to which feelings such as these were at the root of the events of 13 May.

But M. Lacoste could at least put forward the excuse, if indeed it is one, that he had to try and keep pace with events. He may even have felt that there was something tragic in his position as

Minister of Torture. He summed up his position one day by saying, 'I am like a rat in a trap.' The machine might grind on in Algiers but it was in Paris that the parts of the machine were manufactured.

The first part produced was the emergency legislation. From the outset, the Algerian war was classified as subversion under Common Law. A law of 3 April 1955, which had been drafted by the Government of M. Mendès-France, and strengthened and voted by that of M. Faure, authorized the Government to declare a 'state of emergency' in more than one department simultaneously. It was not long before this law had been brought into force over the entire territory of Algeria. As a result, procedures forbidden by law became permissible: house searches at night; censorship of the Press; transfer of terrorist cases to Military Tribunals; and confinement orders which, in practice, meant imprisonment in detention camps. The law on the state of emergency could not continue in force in the event of dissolution of the National Assembly which occurred on 2 December 1955; but it was immediately extended by a decree authorizing the Governor-General to take exceptional measures provided that these were duly reported.

This emergency legislation at least had the advantage of calling a spade a spade. But this could not be said of the law of 16 March, which an almost unanimous National Assembly, including the Communists, voted on 12 March. It was actually entitled 'Law authorizing the Government to put into force in Algeria a programme of economic expansion and giving the Government powers to take any exceptional measures necessary to re-establish order, to protect persons and goods, and to safeguard the territory.' It was that part of the law referring to 'social progress' which persuaded all parties to swallow the 'special powers', as they came to be called, which were kept in force by every Government of the Fourth and Fifth Republic. By virtue of these special powers, a decree of 17 March 1956 gave to the Minister Resident (in the words of M. C. A. Colliard, Dean of the Law Faculty in Grenoble) 'true dictatorial power such as no servant of the State or Minister of the Republic has ever had'. In particular, the Decree of 17 March authorized M. Lacoste 'to issue a confinement order in respect of any person whose activities prove to be dangerous to security or public order'. At first the civil authority used this power with comparative moderation; although between 17 April 1956 and 7 January 1957, 1,500 confinement orders were issued in the old department of Algiers, only 800 were confirmed. But after the decree of 7 January, which gave police powers to General Massu, a confinement order was little more than a piece of paper, giving the bureaucrats the opportunity of checking the number of random arrests made by the military authorities.

The special powers and the emergency legislation did not give rise to the practice of torture. But they were in large measure brought into force, not merely to assist in putting down terrorism, but to meet the requirements of the torturers. When the war in Algeria broke out, the French Authorities had a choice between two policies: either to admit that a fundamental political question was at the root of the Algerian problem, or to decide that this problem could be solved by military and police methods. The adoption of the emergency legislation meant that the Government, and with it the National Assembly, had chosen the second alternative and had, in fact, surrendered to the torturers. Instead of increasing its authority the State had embarked upon a process of self-destruction. The police and later the military became its only representatives. The special legislation established a direct link between the Head of the State and the users of the water and electrical tortures.

The emergency legislation was only one stone among many in the edifice of self-deception and untruth which was gradually being constructed. 'Algeria is France' had already been the cry of Ministers in the Government of M. Mendès-France and of the Prime Minister himself, though the latter had at least uttered some truths which were later to cost him dear. M. Faure, that skilled tight-rope walker in the Parliamentary game, did his best to avoid dealing with the problems of North Africa, although, by a series of unhappy and complicated manoeuvres, he managed to conclude the Franco-Tunisian agreement and to precipitate the return of the Sultan of Morocco. But the problem of Algeria was far graver, and M. Faure was a pawn in the game rather than a player. He left it to his Minister of the Interior, M. Bourgès-Maunoury, to initiate the suppression of newspapers ('no call-up for your war' wrote Claude Bourdet when the first reservists were called up) and to mount the rostrum of the National Assembly in order to tell the colossal lies which were to become so fashionable. When a Communist deputy from Oran, Madame Sportisse, made a series of accusations, the Minister had the audacity to reply:

Madame Sportisse should not assume that my silence yesterday in face of her long list of atrocious inaccuracies implies that they in any way accord with the facts which have been reported. All I can do here is to dispute the accuracy of the statements which have been made from this rostrum but at the same time assure her that each case will be or has been thoroughly investigated. What I can say is that according to the inquiries so far carried out, I have no knowledge of any act of torture bearing any resemblance to those which have been mentioned.

The man who made these categorical statements had already been in possession of M. Wuillaume's Report and M. Mairey's first report for some time.

The electoral campaign which opened as a result of the dissolution of the Chamber on 2 December 1955 was coloured by a vague yearning for 'peace in Algeria'. This was falsely represented as being easily achieved; and the very meaning of the word 'peace' in this context was far from clear since any reference to independence for Algeria was avoided. Torture and the various oppressive measures connected with the war were not a central issue in the campaign. However on 29 December, in order to make the French people aware of something which the outside world had long known, Jean Daniel published in *L'Express* a report giving a detailed description of a summary execution illustrated by a series of photographs which had already been published in October in *Life* magazine. Government circles explained that 'some days after the bloody events of 20 August 1955, a Fox Movietone reporter had bribed a supplementary reservist gendarme who was guarding some of the people involved in the massacres in the department of Constantine. In order to get a news film, he had persuaded this gendarme to shoot one of the prisoners. Both the gendarme and the reporter were guilty of a criminal act.' The Government moreover let it be known that it had only been informed of this incident through the foreign Press, that the gendarme would be court-martialled, and that a charge would be brought against the cameraman for bribing a public servant. This was an odd explanation when we remember that it is now well known that on the day after 20 August prisoners had been executed in hundreds; but the Government had already reached the stage of explaining away what it could not hide.

M. Mollet, who then came to power, turned this policy of deception into a veritable institution; but for our purposes, the personality of this man, who was the outward and visible sign of a general attitude of mind, matters little. The war in Algeria was at that time really unpopular only with a limited number of the young men who had to fight in it, and M. Mollet, faced with extremist opposition, felt that it was the extremists who were the real power in the country. He accordingly chose to carry on with the war and, because he was a man of the Left, he was able to drag or lead the people as a whole into the war. Only a few conscripts gave vent to noisy but ephemeral opposition. The recall of the reservists raised no serious opposition from any political quarter.

The war in Algeria had to go on, so public opinion kept silent in spite of the reports of torture; but when necessary people even muzzled themselves. In *Le Monde* of 5 April 1956, the historian Henri Marrou wrote:

During the last two or three weeks a curious lethargy has come over public opinion, or rather those who are responsible for expressing public opinion. Before the introduction of the special powers the Press and radio were threatened with a 'measure of control', and it seems that their reaction has been to impose strict self-discipline upon themselves. As a result, we now have once more to start listening to the Swiss radio and we have to rely on the foreign Press for our information. It is through these channels that the most important items of news reach us, and they are met by no official reaction other than an embarrassed silence.

Such pronouncements were few and far between in 1956; Henri Marrou was visited by the police because in his article he had characterized torture, summary executions, and collective reprisals as crimes. A few weeks later, on 17 June 1956, the President, René Coty, speaking at Verdun, replied in his own inimitable manner:

'Down there in Algeria our country is in danger, our country is fighting. Our duty is therefore simple and clear. The country commands those who are not subject to military discipline to exercise the essential minimum of civil discipline and to refrain from *any act or even any word* liable to sow doubt in the minds of the sons of our country whom the Republic has called to arms in order that these abominable acts of violence may be brought to an end by the might of France which is inseparable from the generosity of France.'*

In fact, the better type of Frenchman did keep his mouth shut. Much later, in April 1957, Jean-Marie Domenach, the Editor of *Ésprit* explained why he had done so in an article entitled 'The Demoralization of a Nation'. He wrote:

For months we have published no eye-witness accounts from Algeria: not because they were not available: nor because we are afraid of them. Ten years ago we gave full publicity to the acts of injustice and the atrocities which we felt were bound to cause revolt. But once the war had begun, we felt that the most effective method of putting an end to these iniquities was negotiation. In view of the campaign which the outside world was conducting against France, we should, if we had continued to denounce the atrocities committed by our troops and our police, have been helping our opponents' propaganda, and rubbing salt into the wound of our humiliation at home. We would thus have been postponing that peace which we want above all. This is what we believed. As a matter of expediency, therefore, we have temporarily given up publishing these reports. We handed over many of the documents we possessed to the Military Authorities, but they have produced no reaction.

The Mollet Government contrived to persuade the general public to maintain this silence without having recourse to any particularly severe measures. Some arrests were made, but no one was kept under detention for long; Claude Bourdet, Robert

* The day after this speech, the President of the Republic authorized the first execution of two Algerian members of the F.L.N. and so set in motion the chain of events which led to the Battle of Algiers – see Chapter 3 above.

Barrat, and André Mandouze were arrested; some newspapers were seized and some journalists and militant members of the Opposition were charged with 'attempts to demoralize the army'. But there was no need for any tougher methods, for in general the country, as the by-elections showed, toed the line.

Nevertheless, conscripts were present at, or took part in, many atrocious scenes of torture, and their reports, generally forwarded by Socialist friends in Algeria, began to pile up on the Prime Minister's desk. The vast majority of these reports remained secret in 1956 – only one exploded. In September it was learnt that certain European militant Communists had been atrociously tortured in the cellars of the Treasury in Oran where the Super Prefect had ordered them to be 'confined'. The Government employed its well-tried stratagem of implicating in its own web of deception the greatest possible number of apparently highly respectable people and institutions. A journalist from *Le Figaro* was allowed to interrogate the victims. He returned with a sceptical report, published on 10 October and entitled 'I Saw the Victims of Torture in Oran'. In this report, however, he gave a long description of the technique of the electrical torture. A commission of inquiry, including representatives of all parties except the Communists, was set up by the National Assembly. Its President was the Socialist M.P. and Mayor of Roubaix, M. Provo, a personal friend of the Prime Minister. With the single exception of Dr Hovnanian, who was also the only medical member, the Commission returned in March 1957 with a report which paid tribute to the police, recognized the 'moving statements' of the accused, but concluded that they were false. The Commission, however, produced not a shred of evidence to support their conclusions; their report was little more than an act of faith in the rectitude of the police and the reasons they gave for their confidence in the police were singularly pragmatic. The following is the actual conclusion of the report:

The Defence holds to the argument that 'There is no smoke without fire'. But there is doubt; there is always doubt. How are men to be found to carry on in conditions such as these the exhausting job which circumstances have made necessary? How can we recruit for a profession which has to serve the country in such atrocious conditions?

The search for the truth frequently brings us into conflict with the arguments of the parties involved in the case. We have been careful to avoid the trap of being overcome by doubts [sic] since, in that case, we should never have reached a conclusion. After an exhaustive examination of documents, the Commission, with one exception, came unanimously to the conclusion that nothing in the inquiry which it had carried out could lead it to conclude that torture had been used.

In the first quarter of 1957 the Government began to realize that its standard of deception was not good enough. The reservists were returning and some of them had published a pamphlet entitled *Des Rappelés témoignent* (*Some Reservists Bear Witness*); Pierre Henri Simon had published *Contre la torture* (*The Case against Torture*), and in April *Ésprit* published Robert Bonnaud's shattering eye-witness account entitled *La Paix des Nementchas* (*The Peace of Nementcha*) in which the following appeared:

If the honour of France can only be vindicated through torture, then France is a nation without honour. A few Frenchmen were tortured in Oran and hundreds of Algerians are being tortured all over the country every day. Moreover the practice of torture, though perhaps not the present methods used, dates, not from the summer of 1956 nor even from November 1954; it dates from the moment when natives of Algeria and the forces of law and order, Arabs and policemen, found themselves together in Algeria.

Jean-Jacques Servan-Schreiber, with the open support of General de Bollardière, published his memoirs in serial form in *L'Express* under the title *Lieutenant en Algérie*. Cardinals, Archbishops, and the Protestant churches began to talk. M. Lacoste however persisted in his campaign of deception, giving vent to a series of truculent remarks about those who denounced the torturers; at one moment he referred to 'intellectual and sentimental exhibitionists', at another to 'Operation Conscience' and on 21 March he shouted in the Assembly:

'What are we to think of a Muslim lawyer, a leading lawyer too [Ahmed Boumendjel], who accuses the security forces of having driven one of his Algerian colleagues [Ali Boumendjel] insane by the treatment he received, when the facts are that the man supposed to have been the victim of this horrible treatment first attempted to commit suicide and was then merely made subject to a confinement order?'

Two days later it was learned that Ali Boumendjel had 'committed suicide'. René Capitant, a Professor of Law and an ex-Minister, suspended his course of lectures in protest.

It was clear that falsehood pure and simple was becoming impossible. No sooner had the Minister of National Defence accused witnesses of being accomplices in the crimes which they reported 'in that they had not informed the authorities to whom they were responsible', than he received a letter from the Dean of the Faculty of Law in Algiers, M. Peyrega, describing a summary execution;* no sooner had he announced that General de Bollardière had resigned his command 'for family reasons' than the General publicly gave out the real facts. M. Mollet was cleverer, and even pretended a show of emotion. 'The Government itself wants the truth', he cried one day when answering questions on the Boumendjel affair. He denied nothing but he tried to minimize everything.

'We must be unequivocal about this [he declared on 14 April to a meeting of supporters of the Socialist Federation in the Department of the Marne].There have no doubt been certain deplorable acts of violence but they have been extremely rare; and I can assure you that they have been committed only in the heat of battle or in anger at terrorist atrocities. As for premeditated, deliberate torture, I say that if that existed, it would be an intolerable situation. In this connexion the behaviour of the French Army has been compared to that of the Gestapo. This is a scandalous comparison. Hitler issued directives prescribing the use of barbarous methods, whereas the orders which Lacoste and I have issued have always been exactly to the contrary. Inquiries have been ordered and sentences awarded in punishment of some disgraceful acts, but I repeat – the number of cases of this nature can be counted almost upon the fingers of one hand.'

M. Pineau, the Minister of Foreign Affairs, followed the same line at the United Nations. In a speech on 4 February he characterized the accusations made against France as 'fantastic' and the incidents cited as trivial, although they were in fact cases upon which M. Mairey's two reports had given the Government

---

* When this letter was published M. Peyrega's colleagues demanded and obtained the agreement of the Minister of National Education to his suspension.

the most detailed information proving that they were actually extremely serious.

In order to calm people down, M. Mollet set up a 'Commission for the safeguarding of individual rights and liberties',* consisting of a number of eminent personalities. Public opinion was gradually reassured; for the technique had now been perfected. It was only when *La Question* by Henri Alleg was published on 12 February 1958, and suppressed on 27 March, that the discussion was seriously reopened. However, by ensuring that the measures taken against this type of publication never reached the stage of legal action, M. Mollet and his successors managed to keep criticism within tolerable limits.

In any case, other more discreet methods of defeating the anti-torture campaign were to hand. In a letter to the Archbishop of Paris, M. Mollet threatened to cut off the subsidy to the Catholic Schools because a priest had had the temerity to send him documentary evidence in support of his reports of torture. It was in the *Review of Military Information*, published by M. Lejeune's staff, that the specialists in subversive warfare published their counter-terrorist theories. Thus the State was now subsidizing precisely the men who had filled it with such a sense of power. But M. Mollet did even better. In June 1957 a Paris publisher, Éditions Grasset, published a small book entitled *Contre-poison ou la morale en Algérie* (*Antidote or Morality in Algeria*) which was intended to put a spoke in the wheel of the anti-torture campaign. The author, M. Michel Massenet, summarized his aim in these words: 'To make Robert Barrat, Jean-Jacques Servan-Schreiber, and Charles André Julien keep their mouths shut.' He had received a subsidy of 500,000 francs released from the Secret Service vote by M. Mollet, who had read and personally annotated the manuscript. A way was found of surreptitiously indicating to the military that the book represented the views of the authorities by publishing selected pages from it in the *Review of Military Information* side by side with the pronouncements of M. Mollet quoted above.

'What we are doing here, we shall do in France. What we are

* For the activities of this Commission, see Chapter 5.

doing to you, we shall do to your Duclos and your Mitterrands and we shall blow sky-high your whore of a Republic.' These, according to Henri Alleg, were the words of Lieutenant Erulin during one of his torture sessions.

From whatever aspect one considers the problem of torture, as it presented itself in 1954 and 1958, one is brought back to 13 May. The men in Paris who, from 1956 onwards, were working for a change in the régime and the installation of a strong Government, whether under General de Gaulle or someone else, were in close contact with the counter-terrorist organizations in Algiers, which themselves were in contact with the military. It is therefore not surprising to find M. Debré and M. Soustelle in particular, getting into contact via M. Pascal Arrighi with Dr Kovacs, who was responsible not only for the bomb attack on the Casbah (end of August 1956) but also for the attempted bazooka assassination of General Salan (16 January 1957). The only reason why in 1957 the plotters became more discreet and the connexions between those involved somewhat looser, was to avoid embarassing the Army now it had been given full power in Algiers.

The plots were renewed after the dramatic events at Sakhiet Sidi Youssef,* when the Government again backed up the Military Authorities but this time with some reluctance. The 'good offices' of Mr Murphy and Mr Beeley, the Anglo-American mediators, looked like the forerunner of capitulation. On 10 May 1958 M. Chaban-Delmas, Minister of Defence in M. Gaillard's Government which had just resigned, and one of the most active of the plotters, visited Algeria and addressed a group of officers in these words:

'In my view if we fail here, there will be no French Army because there will be no France. All we require is sufficient determination; there is no need to worry as far as equipment is concerned; you now have 440,000 men: if the next Government continues where we have left off and keeps the conscripts with the colours, then you will have 480,000 men against 20,000 rebels; one frontier is to all intents and purposes watertight already and the other can soon be made so if necessary.

* A Tunisian village near the frontier of Algeria which was bombed on 8 February 1958 by French airmen who claimed in justification that they were destroying artillery firing into Algerian territory.

Matters are in your hands and in those of your commanders. Nothing can deter the French Army from being the main pillar of the nation: if it does, gentlemen, we shall weep tears of blood.'

To whom was this militant and prophetic speech addressed? To the officers of the anti-guerrilla school commanded by Colonel Bigeard, the school where torture was part of the curriculum.

CHAPTER 5

The Period of Injustice

THE reader may be excused for thinking it a waste of time to try
to show how the French judicial system in Algeria worked during
the rebellion. The Courts in Algeria had, in fact, arrived at the
cross-roads between two types of legal procedure: on the one
hand, the law of the 'special powers' which resulted in the majority
of those accused being held under arrest for long periods before
being brought before an Examining Magistrate; on the other
hand, that of the code of common law under which this practice
is absolutely forbidden. It has already been shown that a similar
state of affairs existed in embryo before the war in Algeria started,
since it was the police who conducted inquiries. The law which
instituted the state of emergency made it easier, and the Decree of
17 March 1956, made it obligatory to remove from the jurisdiction of the Courts of Common Law any misdemeanour or crime,
even down to a case of indecency, if it had been committed after
31 October 1954. These were not the only consequences of the
special powers. The majority of Muslim lawyers were 'confined'
in internment camps where conditions were such that the Bar of
Algiers, even though the majority of its members were extremists,
felt it necessary to protest. The President of the Algiers Bar told
the following typical story to the Chairman of the 'Safeguards
Commission', who included it in the Commission's Report:

A young barrister in pupillage, Menouer Omar, had clearly been paying
little attention to his lectures. So the Chairman sent for him, admonished
him, and officially assigned him to the defence of a terrorist Menouer
did what he was told. But two days later he was arrested and interned
in the camp at Lodi.

After the decree of 7 January 1957 and the assumption of full
powers by the military, the normal processes of law were, in fact,
disregarded completely. M. Reliquet, Director of Public
Prosecutions in Algiers from October 1956 to September 1958,

76

was reduced to dealing with briefs, the files of which contained nothing but newspaper cuttings. He actually wrote to M. François Mitterrand, Minister of Justice in the Government of M. Mollet: 'I regret to have to inform you that the Press is now the main, if not the only, source of information for the Public Prosecutor's office in Algiers.' A circular from General Allard dated the 20 April laid down that 'names of those placed in confinement will only be given to the Public Prosecutor under secret cover', but immediately afterwards the circular adds that cases will 'only be passed to the Courts with the agreement of the Military Authorities'.

From top to bottom the machinery of the law was kept in ignorance. On 2 April 1957 M. Mitterrand was questioned by the Judicial Committee of the National Assembly. He could do little more than protest his good intentions, and for the rest, refer his questioners to M. Lacoste: 'During the last two months the Civil Courts in Algiers have only had before them seventeen cases involving thirty-nine persons. These thirty-nine persons were brought before the Algiers Courts by the police or gendarmerie within the legal time-limit. I am therefore fully responsible to you only for these thirty-nine counts in seventeen legal cases.'

In such circumstances, it was no good expecting the legal system in Algeria to be capable of putting an end to the use of torture. The victims were often unwilling to bring forward a complaint in the understandable fear that reprisals would be taken against them or their families. Children were known to have been murdered because their brothers or fathers had laid a complaint of torture. In some cases, although the marks of torture were obvious, the Public Prosecutor was unable to persuade the victim to lay a complaint even after he had visited the prisoner personally, and it would have been more than his own life was worth to make an official report on the subject. Even so a few charges were made, but, since most of the torturers were military personnel, these charges were initially brought before Military Courts. An order for investigation into thirty-one incidents was signed on 20 April 1957. Maître Maurice Garçon, the Secretary General of the 'Safeguards Commission' and a leading barrister, examined the record at the beginning of June, and wrote:

We could only note with astonishment that, although the Military Courts had clearly been informed of these matters, for briefs had been prepared, they had apparently done nothing to try to discover the facts of the cases.

He noted further that a military doctor only started to examine the fifteen plaintiffs 'more than two or three months after the incidents in question'. He continued:

In the case of Pascaud, no medical opinion was ever asked for despite his statement that the arch of his temple had been so broken by blows that pinning was necessary, which would certainly have left a mark.

He added:

The examining magistrate appears so far to have done nothing whatsoever. The only instrument of investigation which we found recorded was the dispatch to Paris of a rogatory commission to find out from M. Duverger, a member of the staff of *L'Express*,* the source of the information published in an article of 5 April.

Later, however, officers of parachute units and their victims were brought face to face in court. The officers simply stated that their orders were to treat those under detention with the utmost courtesy. Such encounters may have angered the officers concerned, but they can hardly be said to have served the cause of justice.† Only a very small minority of the cases of torture which actually occurred, therefore, were brought before the Military Courts. One case, however, was brought before the Civil Courts – that of Maurice Audin, who was a European, a university graduate, and a Communist. On 4 July 1957, Madame Audin brought a charge of culpable homicide against X, thus avoiding the necessity of citing the names of the military personnel concerned. The military authorities said that Audin had escaped by jumping from a jeep while being transferred from one place of

---

* M. Maurice Duverger is on the staff of *Le Monde* and *L'Express* and is at the same time Professor of the Faculty of Law in Paris.

† The following story is characteristic. The General-Commissioner for the city of Algiers, M. Builles, heard one day that his Muslim chauffeur's nephews had been murdered and their bodies burnt. He instituted an inquiry and identified the culprit who was an officer of the Foreign Legion. He could get no legal redress.

confinement to another. This was the story which the civil Examining Magistrate, M. Bavoillot, an outspoken supporter of torture, set out to prove with an energy worthy of a better cause. It was several months before he could be persuaded to hear the testimony of Henri Alleg, who had been under detention at the same time as Maurice Audin. On 7 January 1958 the Examining Magistrate ordered a 'reconstruction' of the 'escape' of Audin. One has only to read the official record to realize that the reconstruction was staged by Lieutenant Charbonnier, the very man who later turned out to be the murderer.

In the vast majority of cases, therefore, the torturers were not brought to justice. On the few occasions when the full legal procedure was followed by the Military Courts, this took place in complete secrecy, indeed if even a single name appeared in the Press the culprit was assured of getting off scot free; and any sentences awarded were in any case ludicrously small. The only persons who were really tried were those who had fallen foul of their superiors for reasons other than the crimes in question. M. Christian Pineau gave the following information to the United Nations:

A report produced by the Judge Advocate's office on 22 December 1956 shows that seventy-four cases have been brought before the special tribunals. The vast majority of these cases are of very minor importance.

Louis Martin-Chauffier, an author who conducted an inquiry for the International Commission for the suppression of concentration camps, was able to see a list, dated June 1957, of the sentences which had been passed. They were 'fewer than a hundred and the heaviest was no more than thirty days' imprisonment'.*

But while the torturers escaped justice, sentences were continually being passed on other men in Algeria: active members of the F.L.N., M.N.A., or Algerian Communist Party, or mere suspects with no political affiliation who, through some chance denunciation, had landed in prison. In the ordinary course of events, commitment to prison carries with it some form of

* *Saturn*, January–March 1958.

security; it guarantees the prisoner against torture either by the military or the police. But in Algeria this was true in principle only. At the trial of certain Communist members of the medical profession in 1957, Jacques Salort, an ex-administrator of the daily newspaper *Algér Républicain* was cited as a witness. The *Écho d'Alger* reported: 'He was carried, or perhaps it would be better to say supported, into the witness-box by two policemen.' Salort showed the Court marks of torture on his forearms, but in spite of this two lawyers pressed the magistrates to send him to prison. Salort was sent back into the hands of the police. So even the Examining Magistrates were not above collaborating with the torturers. At Philippeville in November 1955 one of the magistrates saw nothing objectionable in interrogating those due to appear before him in their cells, miserable holes measuring no more than 3 ft 6 ins. × 7 ft 8 ins. × 2ft 6ins.* It goes without saying that no lawyer was present at these extraordinary interrogations. If the accused showed any hesitation in repeating his confession before the Examining Magistrate, the latter usually sent him back to the police or the military. On 5 January 1957, for example, M. Catherineau, the Examining Magistrate who later heard the cases of Henri Alleg and Djamila Boupacha, authorized Yahia Briki to be taken from prison and handed over to the team of torturers headed by Superintendent Redonet. One Examining Magistrate at Constantine interrogated a witness who was in such a state of injury and exhaustion that he fainted in the Magistrate's office; this did not, however, prevent the latter forcing him to sign a confirmation of his confession. Another magistrate, M. Bavoillot, in charge of the Djamila Bouhired case, was accused by the defendant of writing blatant falsehoods into the record in the shape of confessions which had never been made.

It must be obvious that confessions extracted under these conditions were hardly sound evidence in law. The *Écho d'Alger* of 6 March 1957 carried the following article:

The investigation carried out by the First Foreign Legion Parachute Regiment (Green Berets),which led to the arrest of Badeche Ben Hamdi, the murderer of M. Froger (Chairman of the Federation of Mayors of

* This is mentioned in M. Mairey's second Report.

Algiers and a leading extremist) was delayed by a devilish stratagem on the part of the F.L.N. killers. In order to cover the real culprit, complicate the job of the parachute troops, and create confusion, four or five of them all confessed to this crime.

At his trial Badeche steadfastly denied that he was guilty saying: 'You may be able to bend a bar of iron but you cannot bend a man.' He was nevertheless condemned to death and executed. He was undoubtedly innocent for shortly after his execution, it was announced by Algiers radio that the 'real culprit' – yet another – had been killed after a regular siege operation. In any event it now seems certain that the Froger murder was in fact a provocative action by extremists.

In these conditions the processes of law are more akin to a ceremonial ritual – one might almost say ritual murder – than justice. The case of Djamila Bouhired is the best-known example, but there are many others. It was useless for the accused to try to help their case by describing the tortures to which they had been subjected. At the trial of a group of Oran intellectuals Evelyn Lavalette, a leader of the Catholic Action group, brought medical proof that she had been tortured, but the Public Prosecutor, M. Bousquet, merely replied with a chuckle: 'We are not here to try St Evelyn the martyr but Evelyn Lavalette, an accomplice of murderers.'*

Interrogations invariably included physical violence. During one of the bomb-attack trials, General Salan's legal adviser, Colonel Gardon, who was also a Government Commissioner but had never made any bones about his belief that strong-arm interrogation was essential to the furtherance of pacification, called for 'a legal authority with teeth'. Meanwhile justice had been so debased that, to protect their clients, lawyers would often appeal to public opinion, refuse to put forward a defence, and leave the Court.

Sentences were invariably severe, sentence of death being

---

* Any attempt to make a case of having been tortured to the Courts in Algiers generally made matters worse, though the Christian Progressives, who were tried in July 1957, were given light sentences as the result of a deal between the Defence and the Prosecution by which if the Defence made no mention of torture, the Prosecution would not ask for heavy sentences.

inflicted for every kind of reason. Fernand Yveton, for instance, was an active Communist who placed a bomb, but he had been careful to ensure that it would cause material damage only: for this he was executed. Finally, sentences were never submitted to the Court of Appeal but only to a Military Appeal Tribunal which, it was thought, could produce more rapid results.

If the dates on which executions were carried out are compared with those on which political events took place, it seems clear that the President of the Republic granted or refused mercy (mercy is granted much more frequently in France than in England) for reasons which had nothing to do with justice. Heads fell when there was some particular reason to placate the extremists. The highest authority of the State therefore seemed to be ranging itself behind these extremely questionable legal procedures.* The pretext for the demonstration of 13 May 1958 was the execution of three French soldiers by the F.L.N. Yet there were few either in Algeria or in France who were able to see that, vile though it was, this murder was no worse than the numerous executions which had taken place in Algiers without protest from anyone, and that the F.L.N. were merely retaliating.

Under the ancient régime, before 1789, there existed extraordinary tribunals which formed no part of the regular legal system and were intended to cater for cases in which the latter proved ineffective. These tribunals consisted of judges specially appointed by the King who were dispatched into the country to hear grievances and to re-establish the authority of the State in one of its most vital spheres, that of dispensing justice. The people called these extraordinary assizes 'The Great Days'. One such assize was held at Clermont between 26 September 1665 and 30 January 1666, of which there exists this historical account:

More than 12,000 grievances were brought before it and a vast number of cases, both civil and criminal, were heard. In the case of the latter, the occupants of the dock were surprising. Among the accused were many who for reasons of birth, rank, or riches were held to be some of

* In this paragraph on the legal system, I have made much use of Paul Thibaud's excellent study entitled 'Comment fonctionne la justice en Algérie', *Esprit*, May 1957.

the most important personages in the Auvergne and neighbouring provinces. Even judges and priests appeared.

The Auvergne had for years been fleeced by the local nobility who, as a result of various upheavals, had contrived to make themselves completely independent of the central Government. By re-establishing the rule of law, such as it was in those days, the 'Great Days' of the Auvergne re-established the regular order of things at least for the time being. The folksongs of the district carried on the memories of these courts for many years.

Undoubtedly the announcement on 5 April 1957 by M. Mollet's Government of the setting-up of a permanent commission to safeguard individual rights and liberties produced an effect analogous to that of the proclamation of a 'Great Day' session under the the old régime. The guilty were uneasy; hope revived among the victims of oppression, at least among those who had not already lost all belief in French justice; those who had protested, hitherto in vain, against the methods employed by the forces of repression breathed a sigh of relief. At last the truth would be known. This was the general reaction of the liberal press which toned down its campaign (which had not been very energetic anyway).

When he solemnly invested the Commission with its functions on 10 May M. Mollet was quite explicit. He said,

It is the Government's intention that your Commission should be completely independent. It will be your duty to elect your Chairman, to decide on your rules of procedure, and on the type and amount of equipment which you feel you should have available. It will also be your duty to decide the extent of the powers that you consider to be necessary in order to carry out your task in its entirety. The Government will grant you these powers without any hesitation.

Although some declined the honour offered to them, the members of the Commission were men who were eminent in their fields. A Judge of the Cour de Cassation, M. Pierre Beteille, who was elected Chairman, a Warden of the University (M. Pierre Daure), an honorary Governor General of the Colonial Service (M. Robert Delavignette), an ambassador (M. André François

Poncet), Maître Maurice Garçon of the Académie Française, the President of the Bordeaux Bar (Maître Moliérac), an ex-Judge Advocate General (M. Marcel Oudinot), the President of the French Association of ex-Service Men (Émile Pierret-Girard), Professor Charles Richet an ex-inmate of Buchenwald and a member of the Academy of Medicine, Professor de Vergejoul, Chairman of the National Committee of Medical Practitioners, General Henri Zeller, the Military Governor of Paris, and M. Paul Haag, an ex-Prefect of the Department of the Seine. On the face of it, it was unlikely that men of this standing would allow themselves to be hoodwinked.

Nevertheless, the circumstances surrounding the setting up of the Commission ought to have raised questions in people's minds. When announcing the formation of the Commission, the Cabinet had been careful to link it with 'an indignant protest against the campaign organized by the enemies of France seeking to show that our Army and our Civil Government in Algeria are systematically employing methods of repression which contravene the rules of respect, of persons'. The Cabinet declared further that they understood 'because they shared them, the sincere feelings of those who hoped that any individual who failed to follow the steadfast policy of France, the very basis of which is the rights of the individual, should be unmasked and punished'. The same communiqué made known that it was M. Lacoste, M. Lejeune, and M. Bourgès-Maunoury who had proposed the formation of the Commission, and it was well known that it was these very three Ministers who had been the most opposed to any control over the forces of repression. Last but not least, unlike the 'Great Days', the Commission was to hold all its sessions in secret and its reports were to be submitted to the Government alone. A balanced and unemotional appraisal of the value of the Safeguards Commission can now be made. The main documents which it produced have been published, not, indeed, by the Government but in *Le Monde*, which was enterprising enough to publish the Commission's summary report.*

There is no doubt that most of the members of the Commission had a rather peculiar conception of what they were supposed to

* Edition of 14 December 1957.

do. In August, Professor Richet wrote to an old friend, a fellow-deportee under the German occupation who had let him know how strongly he felt: 'When all is said and done, if it ends in saving someone's life, a crack on the head of a man caught throwing bombs is not so awful as people like to make out.' A crack on the head! It was hardly to be expected that a man who could use that sort of expression, even in private, would have much fellow feeling for the victims of repression in Algeria.

Nevertheless, when visiting the condemned cells in the Barbarossa Prison, Professor Richet and General Zeller did feel some passing pity for their inmates.

There were sixty to sixty-five men waiting there, sometimes up to four or five months, for the moment of execution or mercy; they were packed three at a time into cells built for one or at most two prisoners.

They added:

It should be noted, however, that, according to the prison doctor, the prisoners included some real fanatics who declared that they were proud to die for Algeria. The close quarters in which they were held was a contributory factor to the existence and spread of this spirit of fanaticism.

They concluded:

Finally, we must record that sentences of death are carried out in the prison courtyard according to the law; but in spite of the secrecy maintained, these executions become known to the prisoners and are carried out to the accompaniment of bellowing, shouting, and howling by the women, frequently followed by the men. The prison doctor who was inured to it told us, 'It is a nightmare scene.'

The same members of the Commission had an odd conception of their supervisory functions.

We were housed, fed, and transported by the Resident General [sic – meaning Governor-General!]. Wherever we went we were met with the greatest goodwill and cooperation. Two cars were permanently at our disposal. A convoy, in which we were protected by a fully armed half-platoon in jeeps, made it possible for us to visit Berrouaghia without risk.

It is clear that a visit of this sort was no great secret. Nevertheless, MM. Zeller and Richet wrote as follows:

The secret of our inspection seemed to have been effectively kept, for our arrival seemed to cause general surprise both at Berrouaghia and at Lodi.

In the case of the camps at Lodi and Berrouaghia such lack of forewarning was probably not very serious, since in general terms these camps were well organized; but it was little short of tragic when two members of the Commission made it known that they wished to visit a sorting centre. In fact, they asked Colonel Trinquier (of all people) to designate the centre which they should inspect. The Colonel selected the centre at El-Biar and the visit took place on 19 June. The members of the Commission made no special comment; if they had arrived unheralded they would have found Maurice Audin at the centre, but he, together with Henri Alleg and other prisoners who bore too obvious marks of torture, had been transferred for the day to another locality. Two days later Maurice Audin was murdered. His wife had warned all the authorities, including Professor Richet, but in vain; the latter actually replied to her on 19 June 'The Commission has no power to interpose itself between justice and those under detention or suspect.' This was tantamount to an admission that it was the parachute troops and not the Safeguards Commission who were the representatives of justice. Such an admission was serious, for it meant that these two eminent men were resigned to being used as a cover for torture. But their lack of energy was intentional. M. Teitgen's forceful representations to General Zeller and Professor Richet were toned down in their report to the following: 'The machinery of justice creaks in places.'

This sort of attitude on the part of the members of the Commission was however the exception. In certain cases the Commission was able to collect important documents and information. Most of the documents, for instance the Wuillaume and Mairey Reports, were already in the possession of the Government, which therefore had no need of the Commission to provide it with information. Paradoxically, however, it was in Paris and not in Algiers that the Commission first learnt of the most serious affair with which it had to deal – the suffocation of several dozen Muslims detained in some wine cellars.

Moreover the Commission set certain most peculiar limits to its own inquiry. In principle, it refused to deal with anything which occurred immediately following an operation of war and this effectively gave official blessing to the murder of prisoners. It also in general supported the Government contention that atrocities were the result of errors on the part of individuals. 'Clearly,' wrote the President of the Commission in the Summary Report, 'superior civil and military authority is not necessarily informed of the excesses of which their subordinates are guilty.' The same report emphasizes 'the lofty level of thought' of General Massu. Nevertheless, in a note handed to the Commission on 1 September, M. Teitgen had been quite explicit:

The writer hopes that when he swears on his honour that torture has become current practice, you will not feel it necessary to compel him to bring proof of this fact before you. It is merely necessary for him to assure you that as a result of one year of 'general police duties' he has intimate knowledge of so many files that if he were to draw on his official records, this note would become unreadably long. This is no case of what on 11 March 1957 General Massu called 'smear tactics'. We are well on the way to making torture part of the normal system and seem not to shrink from justifying its use.

But his remarks apparently passed their recipients by.

In general, these distinguished men failed in their task, for they had from the outset accepted an ill-defined task with ill-defined powers. But they were to suffer one more final insult; in spite of the formal undertaking it had given, the Government did not keep the Commission informed of any action taken as a result of its advice and comments – for the very good reason that there was no action.

Thereupon three members of the Commission, Maurice Garçon, Émile Pierret-Girard, and Robert Delavignette, handed in their resignations. Maurice Garçon stated that he was not prepared to let anyone think he could offer protection when in fact he could do nothing. The Governor-General, M. Delavignette, was even more emphatic – and he was no revolutionary nor a supporter of independence for Algeria. As ex-Governor of the Cameroons, he was one of those great viceroys who had once been the pride of the French administration. Clearly he had not seen or grasped everything that went on in Algeria and he showed that he still laboured under certain illusions when he wrote 'in spite of the oppression of the past and their misery in the present, eighty per cent of the Muslims still retain their confidence in French justice, in France, and in a new French Algeria.' But he had grasped one vital fact at least. At the end of 1957 he declared:

'*That which is true for Algeria may very soon be true for France*. Have we sufficiently considered the results when the civil power becomes impotent, when enormous responsibilities are being put into the hands of mere corporals or sergeants? It is frightening to wonder whether mentally they are not turning slowly into policemen. Moreover these groups of paratroopers turned policemen may well not realize what they are doing when *they start using methods which one day may be used elsewhere*. The most serious problem is not the atrocities themselves, but that as a result of them the State is engaged in a process of self-destruction. What we are witnessing in Algeria is nothing short of the disintegration of the State; it is a gangrene which threatens France itself.'

With the hindsight of 1962 M. Delavignette seems to have been no bad prophet. As for the Safeguards Commission which had been inaugurated with such solemnity, it ended by playing almost exactly the role which the Government had intended, it side-tracked rising public indignation. But at the same time it demonstrated yet again that the rulers of France were accomplices in the organization of torture.

Thus neither the ordinary nor the extraordinary system of justice had been able to end methodical torture. Damning records had been compiled, but neither politicians nor magistrates had the courage to let them out into the open. There were records of torture, of counter-terrorism, and of plots, all inextricably tied up with each other. In his capacity as Minister of Justice, M. Mitterrand held a record of the incident of the bazooka attack on General Salan in which were to be found all three – torture, counter-terrorism, and plotting. He used it, however, not to help the official inquiry, but merely as a means of exerting secret pressure on one of his political opponents, M. Debré. On 13 May 1958, when the Fourth Republic finally abdicated, the men who sacked the Central Government building in Algiers, or at any

rate some of them, knew what they were doing. Some were looking for the tax records showing that even at this moment of
'patriotic fervour' they had not lost interest in material matters;
but others, particularly Pierre Lagaillarde, were looking for the
records which implicated them in torture episodes. As for the
record of the bazooka attack, it was ceremonially burnt in police
headquarters in Algiers.

CHAPTER 6

Order and Disorder in the Army

A JOURNALIST who served in the Army in Algeria told the following story of the action taken by General de Gaulle to put down the practice of torture, and the results which this achieved:

When General de Gaulle visited Saida on 27 August 1959, in the presence of M. Delouvrier (who had been appointed Government Delegate-General in Algiers on 19 December 1958) he took Colonel Bigeard aside and ordered him to put an end to the practice of torture. When Bigeard relinquished command of the Saida sector, he collected all his officers together for a luncheon on 29 October 1959; in his after-lunch speech he said (I quote his exact words): 'When General de Gaulle and M. Delouvrier came to Saida, they said to me 'No more torture'. Well gentlemen, I say to you 'No more torture' 'but . . . go on torturing all the same.' He added that General de Gaulle's policies should only be followed when they appeared 'reasonable'.*

This story seems almost symbolic. During the early period of the war in Algeria, many Frenchmen, particularly some serving and reserve officers such as General de Bollardière or General Billotte had come out openly against the practice of torture, and they had been waiting and hoping for a pronouncement on this vital problem from the former leader of the Free French. General de Gaulle had written a number of private letters on the subject, but he had said nothing in public. There was every reason, therefore, when General de Gaulle came back into power for people to expect that he would put an end to these abuses. Nor was this an unreasonable hope as neither revolutionary warfare nor torture had ever featured in General de Gaulle's concept of the military art. His speciality had always been armoured warfare and the most modern methods of war, particularly atomic weapons.

* Gerard Périot, *Deuxième classe en Algérie*, Flammarion, 1962.

Again, the system of torture had started and grown as a result of a number of incidents when the State had surrendered to those who held the real power in Algeria, whether police or military, and there was no doubting General de Gaulle's determination to re-establish the authority of the State. One of his closest collaborators, M. Debré, had told Jean-Marie Domenach, the editor of the left-wing Catholic monthly *Esprit* before 13 May: 'Yes, torture is used in Algeria, because the State has no authority there. When we have a State, then you will see that things will change.' However, the potential conflict between de Gaulle and the disciples of psychological action soon came out into the open.

The situation on 1 June 1958, when General de Gaulle received full powers from the National Assembly, cannot be described in a few simple sentences. In Algeria the 'order' which prevailed was an order of repression; the men who, if they had not started the system of torture, had at least developed it and made it part of the machinery of government, were to be found throughout the official hierarchy. General Salan was Government Delegate-General and in that capacity wielded both the military and civil powers which the Gaillard and Pflimlin Governments had given him. Colonel Godard, the hero of the battle of Algiers, was head of the Sûreté in Algeria; Colonel Trinquier had been appointed Commander of an operational sector; General Massu, the key figure in the whole system, was in charge of the prefecture in the department of Algiers. And this military machine relied for support upon those who had helped to bring it to power: the extremists centred round the Public Safety Committees.

In Paris, the situation was obviously less clear-cut. General de Gaulle's Government included such men as M. Mollet, M. Lejeune, and (from 7 July) M. Soustelle, who had continuously backed up and sometimes even encouraged both the practice of torture and the torturers. M. Jean-Jacques Servan-Schreiber thought he could pick out 'at least three killers' in the National Assembly elected in November, and, in fact, such members as M. Jean-Marie Le Pen, the representative of the Latin Quarter, M. Pierre Lagaillarde, and M. Raymond Vinciguerra, members for Algeria, had personally taken part in torture sessions.*

There were others who, as a result of the various plots designed to destroy the Fourth Republic, had embarrassingly close connexions with the torturers and professional killers. The most noteworthy of these was M. Debré, the Keeper of the Seals (Minister of Justice). On the other hand, there were others who could not conceal their disapproval of these odious practices. On 24 June 1958 one of them solemnly declared: 'I do not know, nor do you, of any act of torture which has been committed since the arrival in Algiers of General de Gaulle. There must be no more of them from now on.' Another, M. Edmond Michelet, who became Minister of Justice, vigorously condemned what he called 'the consequences of the Nazi virus'. This was hardly the way to approach the problem, for the consequences were on an enormous scale.

General de Gaulle himself was silent. One or two phrases, which are probably authentic, have been attributed to him; for instance, 'And now, gentlemen', he is said to have said to a group of officers, 'let the "telephone" be a means of talking to others, not a means of making others talk!' But in public, his rule was silence. All that we can find is what a journalist once called 'a passing reference to the problem of torture'. †

In a speech at Le Havre on 10 July 1960, after the failure of the Melun talks, the Head of the State said,

Today a new Algeria is being formed. We would not have reached this situation – Algeria would have not reached this situation – the world and the peace of the world would not have been safeguarded, had not our army done its duty. I am perfectly well aware that *there may have been some unfortunate incidents and these must be brought to*

* The following story, which I can guarantee is authentic, will give an idea of the moral standards of these representatives of the people. While M. Le Pen was serving in Algeria in a Parachute Unit, he asked a Muslim hotel night-porter in Algiers for a drink. The latter replied that it was after hours and he had not got the key of the cellar. M. Le Pen dragged the porter over to the nearest military post and had him 'interrogated'. There is an official police summary of evidence to support this story which has been published in *Vérité-Liberté*, June–July 1962.

† André Passeron, *De Gaulle parle*, Plon, 1962.

an end, but in general terms, in the main, our soldiers and their commanders have done what they had to do.'

It is doubtful how exactly we should interpret these words. The words 'unfortunate incidents' may have referred to torture or to certain occasions when the Army had disobeyed the civil power and which, on 29 January, during 'the barricades revolt' the General had called '*uncertainty of various military elements*'. We shall probably never know, especially as equivocal phrases like these are in any case characteristic of the General's style. Tributes to the army, and to the 'friendly contacts' which it had 'forged' with the population, were also a constant theme in his speeches.

As a tentative conclusion one might therefore say that the change of régime made no difference, either to the practice of torture or to the implicit 'cover' which the Government afforded it. Indeed, fresh reports of acts of torture came up at regular intervals but led to Government action only at irregular intervals exactly as they had under the Fourth Republic. The Government regularly let it be known that the few excesses which had taken place had been duly punished and no less regularly stigmatized as 'disreputable' those who brought these questions up. But this summary of the state of affairs after 1958, though not entirely wrong, is incomplete and superficial. We must therefore try to see whether today, six months after the signature of the Évian Agreements, it is possible to reconstruct the true march of events.

On 19 December 1958 a new team took over from General Salan in Algeria. It was made up of a civilian, an ex-Inspector of Taxes, M. Paul Delouvrier, who was the brains behind one of the settler pressure-groups (could this be a coincidence?) and an Air Force officer, General Maurice Challe. General de Gaulle published the orders he gave to M. Delouvrier. They contained the following words:

The Government attaches the greatest possible importance to its requirement that all police operations, and all preventive or repressive measures to which these may give rise, should be carried out strictly in accordance with the rules laid down. To this end, commanders are to be held fully responsible for all happenings within the area of their command; no specialist organization, still less any individual, is to act, except on their authority.

Seeing that these orders were written in Paris and addressed to a Civil Servant,* it might be assumed that they were intended to put an end to the uncontrolled system of torture. But out in the country for the last three years the military had made the law and interpreted Government instructions. The three essential phrases in the text quoted above – 'in accordance with the rules', 'responsible' and 'authority' – were to be given an interpretation by the military which probably had not been foreseen by their author.

General Challe adhered strictly to the doctrine of revolutionary war which lays down the principle that 'territorial authority is unquestionably superior to operational authority', and he became a supporter of the theories which had been worked out during the battle of Algiers. So, for men like Colonel Argoud, the moment had arrived to put their theory into practice on the grand scale. The theory of control of the population was systematically applied; 're-grouping' was vastly extended and in the end directly affected more than two million people, primarily women and children, many of whom were threatened with starvation. The Army made great efforts to root out the rebel organization from amongst the population, whatever the cost might be. An official note dated 14 August 1959 from Colonel Renoult, Commander of the 'Batna Sector', summarizes the military outlook fairly adequately.

We must 'keep the population informed' by showing them the advantages of the Constantine plan for the economic development of Algeria. We must also din into their ears by means of talks and individual interviews that there will never be negotiation with the F.L.N. and that 'it will be destroyed down to the last man'.

The destruction of the F.L.N. was the Army's main task and the

---

* Claude Paillat, an extremist right-wing journalist who was generally very well informed, states in his book *Dossier secret de l'Algérie* that M. Delouvrier, when reading out his orders to his subordinates, intentionally omitted this paragraph.

word destruction was no mere verbiage. Colonel Renoult had no hesitation in giving the following orders:

A merciless offensive against the O.P.A. is authorized. Area commanders are empowered not merely to detain, but to liquidate on the spot outlaws carrying on subversive activity and those who wage underground warfare; these include political leaders, collectors of contributions, *merkez* [road guards], informers, secret police, rural constables, members of tribunals, and village head-men.

As a result, a rural constable could, if he belonged to the F.L.N.'s O.P.A., be shot on the spot merely on the decision of an Army captain.

The most original feature of the Challe plan was that this sector organization was backed up by action (coordinated with the actions of the sector forces) on the part of the 'general reserve', usually the parachute troops. These units were allotted to the commanders of the worst 'penetrated' sectors and they acted, in the phrase of an ex-soldier, 'like a steam-roller'.*

The large-scale operations of these units had code-names such as 'Precious Stones' or 'Field Glasses', and they were remarkably destructive. The whole structure of the Algerian countryside was torn to shreds; particularly in the Kabylie, whole villages were destroyed and their inhabitants herded together, tortured, and executed by tens of thousands.

The counterpart to this system was 'Intelligence', or in other words, torture. There was no question of allowing each military unit to develop its own Intelligence technique, as had happened during the first phase of the Algerian war. A single centralized Intelligence organization was felt to be necessary, but at the same time this organization had to be sufficiently de-centralized and widely spread to enable it to 'work' on the spot. The organization was, in fact, ready to hand; it has already been shown how it came into existence in Algiers in 1957. It was called the C.C.I. (Centre de Coordination Inter-Armées – Inter-service Coordination Centre) and to it was attached the D.O.P. (Dispositif Opérationnel de Protection – Operational Protection Organization). These were secret organizations and their names were changed

* Jean-Phillippe Talbo-Bernigaud, 'Rouleau compresseur en Algérie', *Les Temps modernes*, April 1961.

so often that it is sometimes difficult to keep track of them, but we must try. One fact is quite clear; for the Muslims, the name D.O.P. was synonymous with 'torture'. The Red Cross Report for 1960 makes it clear that the majority of the Muslims who presented themselves to the Red Cross Inquiry and complained of torture, had suffered it in a D.O.P. establishment – in other words, in an organization which functioned as an adjunct to the Regular Army and was manned by specialist officers. An ex-conscript has described to me the D.O.P. located in Batna in 1960. It was a large dove-cote situated about twelve miles from the town; round it were to be seen about a hundred graves.

But we must now look at slightly higher echelons. During the years 1958 to 1960, the C.C.I. gradually spread throughout Algeria. This organization was established in Algiers and was autonomous *vis-à-vis* the Joint General Staff; it had, for instance, its own wireless communications. It contained, moreover, officers of all three services, so that any recourse to the Joint General Staff was useless. However, it worked in close cooperation with certain sections of the Army General Staff, in particular the notorious Fifth Bureau; this was in charge of 'psychological action' and on its disbandment after the barricades revolt, was re-named Third Bureau P.H. (Problèmes Humains, Operations Section – Man Management Office).

The C.C.I. consisted of two sections. First there was the C.A.R.O. (Compagnie Administrative de Renseignement Opérationnel – Staff Company for Operational Intelligence), whose primary task was to collect for use in military operations the information produced by the second section. This second section initially had the official title D.O.P. but was later called the D.B.R. (Demi Brigade de Recherche – Intelligence Team). The D.B.R. in its turn spread its tentacles everywhere. At Army Corps and territorial area level (e.g. Algiers, Oran, Constantine, Sahara) it was represented by a battalion which was a purely notional organization. For example, the 157th Infantry Battalion at Constantine and the 61st Infantry Battalion at Oran were the organizations to which, nominally, the Intelligence specialists were posted. In the same way, at zone level (corresponding to an Army division), the D.B.R. was represented by a company, and at sector level by a platoon. In effect, the sector platoon fulfilled the role of the 'Second Bureau' which, in the French Army, is the section of the staff traditionally in charge of Intelligence. In addition all the organizations whose task was to infiltrate the civil population and put down the activity of the O.P.A., also had more or less loose connexions with the D.B.R. Such was the case with the 'Harkas', which in the end comprised nearly 100,000 Algerians, and with the 'information and action centres', a title which, in certain sectors, covered all military and civil police organizations; the outstanding example of such a centre was the notorious Améziane Farm.*

There is no doubt that the commanders of these centres acted on a grand scale; official Deuxième Bureau figures show that between February 1957, when it was set up, and February 1961 Améziane Farm 'dealt with' 108,175 Algerians. Thousands of these were tortured in a building known by the detainees as 'the slaughterhouse', and according to information given to M. Fonlupt-Esperaber, lately an M.R.P. deputy, by several witnesses of unquestionable integrity, more than one thousand had their throats cut.

Parallel with the C.C.I., the Regular Army had its own internment camps which on occasions were also used as places of torture. There were 'sorting and transit centres' in which in theory detainees were held only for a maximum of three months; 'military internment centres' which were used only for prisoners of war; and 'rehabilitation centres' in which the psychological action section tried out its experiments. The civil administration retained control of the shelter camps instituted under M. Soustelle and M. Lacoste.

Looked at through the eyes of the Algerians this was a terrible machine of repression and torture, a straight-jacket designed to

---

* When the name C.R.A. began to have connotations which were too unpleasant other titles were adopted. For instance, at Sidi-Bel-Abbes it was known as G.R.E. (Groupe de Recherche et d'Exploitation – Research and Evaluation Group) and later C.O.M.I.R. (Comité Mixte de Recherche – Joint Research Committee). This alphabetical roundabout was in itself indicative of a state of mind.

keep the Algerian revolution within bounds by terror. From the French Government's point of view the system had the advantage of being relatively secret; the ordinary fighting soldier did not have to know what went on in the buildings of the D.B.R. and could not therefore keep public opinion at home informed, as certain reservists had done in 1957. The government did try by issuing general instructions to put down the 'abuses' which resulted from the system. For instance, in a note of 6 November 1960, General Gouraud, the Constantine Corps and Area Commander, severely criticized 'cases of boorish behaviour, indiscipline, and dishonourable conduct' which had been brought to his notice and threatened that 'should this warning be disregarded', those responsible would be punished 'with the utmost severity'. But although at this time the smooth-running torture establishment at Améziane Farm and its specialist personnel were under his orders, there is no evidence that this warning was ever intended to apply to them. One may well ask, therefore, whether this policy produced concrete results. Several accounts were published, (for instance, Benoist Rey's *Les Égorgeurs**) which showed that some units of the Regular Army were still witnessing or even taking active part in horrifying scenes. Although the authorities had tried to improve matters, they had had only very limited success.

Yet the power they already had was still not enough for the moguls of repression. They wanted a legal system which would be entirely compatible with the methods they used, a legal system which would have the advantages, the privileges, and the authority of the law of the State, and which yet would be as rapid and 'effective' as their own. What they wanted in fact was to legalize summary execution. To a certain extent they got what they wanted. For instance, the sorting and transit centre in the Corniche Casino in Algiers was simultaneously a torture chamber and an interrogation centre for the normal Algiers court. A bitter argument arose between Colonel Argoud and the legal authorities, in particular the Minister of Justice. In 1959 the Chief of Staff of the Algiers Army Corps, who was, not surprisingly

---

* Published in Great Britain by John Calder under the title *The Throat-Cutters*, 1962.

nicknamed 'General Massu's missing brain', set out his requirements in a long note addressed to M. Michelet. The legal system,
he said, should be altered to allow the infliction of punishment,
including sentence of death, not only for acts of terrorism but
also for membership of the O.P.A., which should be considered
tantamount to treason. He also asked that the President's prerogative of mercy and the jurisdiction of the court of appeal should
be suspended. Colonel Argoud gave the following somewhat
emotional account of his interview with the Minister:

I said to him 'Minister, this question of the law is a vital one for the
Army in North Africa, whilst we wrestle with such a dire state of
affairs. I repeat once more, this is more important to us than several
divisions; more important than the odd 100,000 men.' Further to
emphasize my appeal, and to play upon his emotions I said to him:
'I turn to you now not as the Keeper of the Seals but as an inmate of
Buchenwald which to me means that you are a living witness to Nazi
barbarism and the personification of France, which is devoted to the
rights of man.' I said to him: 'Look at the situation in which you place
the French Army. To all intents and purposes you are condemning us to
lose this war and you are perhaps condemning the French Army to
lose its soul!'*

Thus Colonel Argoud was invoking the honour of France and
the rights of man to demand official sanction for the peculiar
system of law which he himself was practising.

In fact some of the senior magistrates on the staff of the
Minister of Justice were just as worried as Colonel Argoud. They
may merely have been making a sincere effort to avoid the further
use of torture by simplifying the ponderous machinery of normal
justice, both civil and military, but they introduced a number of
important modifications in judicial procedure. As an example,
on 12 February 1960 immediately after the revolt of the barricades, a moment when it was clearly necessary to give energetic
support to the Army, a decree was issued eliminating cross-
examination at preliminary hearings in Algeria, forbidding the
briefing of lawyers from France and putting a 'military judge
advocate' in charge of preliminary hearings. These officials were

* Testimony at a hearing *in camera* during the 'barricades' trial, published
in *Sans Commentaire*.

usually magistrates who had been called up for service in a rank junior to that of the sector commander whom they were supposed to keep under control. It was thus possible, in theory, for one of these 'military judge advocates' to say 'henceforth in my sector torture will only be used on my authority'.

An important role in this modification of the legal system to suit the requirements of the war in Algeria was played by the new 'safeguards commission' which rose phoenix-like from the ashes on 13 August 1958. Its chairman was the President of the Criminal Court and of the Cour de Cassation, M. Maurice Patin. In this post M. Patin had the privilege, which he frequently used, of deciding whether certain particularly delicate cases should be transferred to the French courts. But as Chairman of the Safeguards Commission he seemed primarily preoccupied in trying to avoid any outcry; to obtain some improvement perhaps, if possible to ensure that affairs were conducted more in conformity with the law, but mainly to avoid any inopportune action which might cause offence or embarrassment. For instance M. Patin never tried to enter a building in which torture took place: his pretext was that he would have run the risk of being arrested. At the barricades trial Colonel Argoud stated that when M. Patin heard of General Massu's circular giving official blessing to the principle of summary execution he cried:

'I understand completely the terrible position you are in. I understand completely the importance of this problem for the Army, but for God's sake withdraw your directive. You can prepare us all the good briefs you like, you can bring us fake witnesses and I will help all I can, but in God's name withdraw your directive.'

There is no knowing whether this statement was actually made. Although on 11 July 1961 it was M. Patin himself who had to condemn Colonel Argoud to death *in absentia*, he never denied having spoken these words; and of course it is unlikely that he will ever record what he said. What is certain, however, is that those words gave a true indication of M. Patin's thinking and that there was no lack of 'fake witnesses' or 'good briefs'.

Between Paris and Algiers there was a protracted, uneasy balance of concession on the one hand and insubordination on the other. When it thought fit, the High Command in Algiers sabotaged the orders of Paris. On 18 July 1960 M. Pierre Messmer, the Minister of the Armed Forces, presumably thinking that the reform of the legal system in Algeria had met the requirements of the military, issued a circular in which he emphasized his dissatisfaction with 'the abnormal and disquieting number of deaths resulting from attempts to escape during movement of prisoners or operations in which persons under arrest are acting as "guides"'. The Minister requested that cases of 'negligence' or 'neglect of duty' on the part of the commanders responsible should be 'punished with the utmost severity'. General Crépin was at the time Commander-in-Chief in Algeria, but the Minister's order was not passed on until after the arrival of his successor, General Gambiez, whose instruction on the subject was dated 23 March 1961. This means that the order could not have reached area commanders before 11 April at the earliest – in other words, after a delay of almost nine months.

But though Algiers disobeyed Paris, Paris, for its part, did not always give way to Algiers. For instance, the President of the Republic never agreed to give up his prerogative of mercy, although the military leaders constantly pressed him to do so; nor did he agree that the Cour de Cassation should cease to hear appeals against cases heard in Algeria. The right of appeal to the Cour de Cassation in Paris had been suppressed under M. Faure; it was restored under General de Gaulle. Certain important cases, such as the Audin case or the Djamila Boupacha case in 1960, were transferred to civil courts in France, which constituted a grave threat to the military officers involved. On the other hand Paris made many concessions on minor matters; officers who had used torture were awarded decorations and capital punishments were inflicted at psychologically important moments; for instance, on 23 January 1960, just before the revolt of the barricades, M. Delouvrier and General Challe, contrary to all custom, issued a public announcement that three executions would be carried out the following day. On 8 December the Head of the State flew to Algeria where, not unnaturally, he expected a hostile reception from the French element of the population. It was no doubt for this reason, and also to calm down the wilder spirits, that an Algerian and a Moroccan were executed in the courtyard of the Santé Prison in Paris on the very morning the Head of the State was due to leave.

In Algeria, an officer guilty of murder who was arrested might let fall a remark to the effect that some much-decorated commander had committed innumerable murders without being punished for them, and make great play of being ready to denounce him. He would be immediately set free as the price of keeping his mouth shut. Thus the victims of torture were the pawns in this perpetual game of compromise between the Government and 'its' Army.

But the game of compromise could not go on for ever. As soon as it came to power General de Gaulle's Government made great efforts to divorce the Army from the extremists. Vast powers were indeed left with the Army, but on 9 October officers were ordered to resign from the Public Safety Committees. The C.C.I. and the D.B.R. were of course entirely military organizations and were left untouched, but after the crisis of 24 January the territorial units were disbanded; the Fifth Bureau, whose head Colonel Jean Gardes was compromised by his cooperation with the settler insurgents in Algiers, was, in theory at any rate, dissolved; and some semblance of civil authority was gradually re-established in Algiers.*

After the *putsch* of 22 April police powers in Algiers and Oran were no longer in the hands of a general but of a prefect of police. The military organization of repression and in particular the C.C.I. was placed under the control of a mere Colonel and later of a Major. But still its whole subordinate organization remained in being and independent of the normal machinery of government and so still constituted a veritable State within the State.

If this machine had confined its activities solely to action

---

* Torture continued to be used in Algiers but the regimentation of the Muslim population which had hitherto been in the hands of the D.P.U. and the Army became much less severe. It was this that made possible the Muslim demonstrations of December 1960 which would never have been allowed to take place in 1957. Because it felt that it was itself threatened, the Government felt obliged to allow the Muslim population some measure of freedom of expression.

against Muslims the Government would have been satisfied, but any 'state within a state' must have a tendency and indeed a mission towards itself becoming the State, and so the machinery for repression became machinery for plotting. For these men 'pacification' had become a symbol of patriotism. They had no other object in life and they were the holders of fantastic power. They could therefore hardly be expected to accept the direction in which the policy of de Gaulle was turning, the swing towards the ultimate and inevitable independence of Algeria. For some time of course there was no more than verbal fencing, sometimes polished, sometimes crude. When General de Gaulle in Paris talked of 'self-determination', General Massu in Algiers declared that this was only intended for overseas consumption and M. Delouvrier said 'we are fighting for a French Algeria'.

But this game could not go on indefinitely. The military leaders were perfectly well aware that it was impossible to 'integrate' Algeria into France unless a totalitarian régime were established in France, and they were also aware that the necessary economic and political foundations for such a régime did not exist. The French Government gradually realized that there were only two political forces in Algeria – the French Army and the F.L.N., and that unless it wished to see France subjected to a régime similar to that of Algeria, it must at all costs reach agreement with the F.L.N. and give up its dream of creating a third force. The Government did not disown either torture or the torturers, but it gradually brought about a political state of affairs in which negotiation could take place, and as it did so disorder took over within the Army.

In February 1961 a group of exiled officers and Algerian activists formed the O.A.S. around the figureheads of General Salan and Pierre Lagaillarde. This underground organization quickly found the necessary material support in Algeria, from the staff of the C.C.I.; in Constantine, for instance, Major Rodier, the 'squire' of Améziane Farm, became head of the plastic-bomb network. Nothing could show more clearly the fundamental similarity of purpose between the torturer and the plastic bomber. When the 'quartet' of generals and the 'group of ambitious, twisted, and fanatical officers' (General de Gaulle's words) decided to go into action on 22 April 1961, it was through the C.C.I. with its independent radio communications network that the *putsch* was enabled to lay hands without too much difficulty on the vital areas of Algiers. It was the 1st Foreign Legion Parachute Regiment, which had played so decisive a role in the battle of Algiers, which now took over the central government building.

If the *coup* of the 22 April had succeeded, the system of torture would have been enthroned in France itself; but it failed and as a result a real split developed within the apparatus of repression. The O.A.S. then re-established the links between the military and the extremists, made use as far as it could of Colonel Trinquier's techniques of 1957, and organized the European population, making it partially responsible for the 'physical liquidation' of any who opposed it and of the Muslim population without discrimination of any sort. A number of police officers sent from Paris to control the situation were systematically shot down. From the end of 1961 until the agreements of 17 June 1962 between the provisional executive and the Algerian-born members of the O.A.S., a new 'battle of Algiers' raged. Crime ran rife openly in Algiers and in Oran. There were beatings-up, lynchings, kidnappings of suspects, and bomb attacks, which in turn provoked random reprisals. Starting as a 'state within the state' the O.A.S. now indeed began to behave as if it was the State itself. It expelled foreign journalists to whom it took a dislike and it destroyed anything which might give the impression that the real State was still in existence. For instance, on 3 March 1962 it destroyed the Algiers police records. On its side the French Army continued to fight the F.L.N. The torture centres went on functioning right up to the time of the cease-fire and some sections of the Army, for instance the Foreign Legion, continued to use the same methods well after the cease-fire had been announced.

The D.B.R. was not disbanded until 5 April. The auxiliaries also posed quite a problem for they had formed part of the machine of repression and were terrified of the approaching cease-fire: for example, Lieutenant Chesnais commanded a *harka* (auxiliary formation) in the Aurès. His auxiliaries were worried when it was announced that the Évian negotiations would shortly begin, and still more worried when, on 20 May 1961, the

French Government took the unilateral decision to cease offensive operations. Lieutenant Chesnais learnt that his auxiliaries were planning to murder the French members of the garrison and then desert. He could see only one method of restoring discipline; though keeping clear of the affair himself, he authorised his auxiliaries to kill six of his prisoners. In the report which he submitted to his superiors after being placed under close arrest he wrote: 'After this I had my men under control again because it had been proved to them that the F.L.N. had not won the battle and that I was not going to abandon them.'*

Lastly there was a third very much smaller group of officers and police who made it their mission to fight the O.A.S. These were the mobile constabulary in Algiers who had been fired upon by the activists on 24 January 1960; also included were the special police officers offered up in sacrifice by Paris and nicknamed the '*barbouzes*'. There is no doubt that in some cases torture was used on people suspected of belonging to the O.A.S.†

When the cease-fire came into force the machinery of the French State in Algiers had apparently disappeared or at any rate was no more than a façade which the O.A.S. used or disregarded as it liked. Even the announcement of the cease-fire produced no fundamental change. It is true that on 26 March 1962 Army units fired on a crowd of Europeans in the rue d'Isly just as if they had been Muslims; it is true that Bab-el-Oued, the stronghold of the Algiers extremists was cordoned off for several days and searched, though less rigorously than had been the Casbah in 1957; it is true that in Oran General Katz made a short-lived effort to put down the O.A.S.; but in fact over most of the territory of Algeria the Army, as it were, went on general strike and stayed neutral. This attitude almost seemed to hint at some tacit neutrality between the F.L.N. and the O.A.S., the F.L.N. being masters of the country but the O.A.S. heavily

---

* After the Évian agreements, many *harkis* were indeed killed by the F.L.N. and by private-enterprise gangs, some by atrocious means. A few were established in camps in France, but the majority were abandoned in Algeria, even though the reprisals taken against them could easily have been predicted as a consequence inherent in the nature of revolutionary warfare.

† I published complete documentation on this subject in *Esprit*, May 1962.

armed, highly organized, and fully capable of destroying the economy. The agreement of 17 June 1962 resulted in a temporary compromise between these two forces in which the French Government was content to play no more than the role of honest broker. What a humiliating spectacle this compromise was for those who hoped to re-establish the authority of the State in Algeria! Moreover, who could fail to see that by allowing an independent organ of repression, whose favourite weapon was torture, to establish itself and grow, the French Government had prepared the ground for its own disappearance? Indeed the French Government tried to establish order without grappling with the problem of torture and so it not only created disorder but failed to eradicate the practice of torture into the bargain. If it had been possible to restrict the effects of this policy to Algeria, it might have made some sort of sense. But the question which must now be answered is whether the Mediterranean was wide enough to save France from its infectious gangrene.

CHAPTER 7

Gangrene

IN June 1958, General Salan issued what sounded like a challenge ... and a plan of action. He said: 'The Mediterranean runs through France as the Seine runs through Paris.' But since Algeria was not France, was there not a danger that France would become another Algeria – a proving-ground for a police force, and later an army, both determined to use every means, even torture, to achieve their ends? Every time there was a *coup d'etat* or a *putsch*, many Frenchmen seriously feared such an outcome; but what was happening was that France was being 'Algerianized' imperceptibly, day by day.

The original condition of the two countries was very different. The structure of society in France was not colonial, the Muslims in France were not a peasant majority but an industrial minority – at least there were 300,000 Algerians in the worst-paid and least skilled jobs in French industry. In French society the Muslims lived in a world apart, so much so that in 1952 a doctor (Frantz Fanon) who had many Algerian patients could write of a 'North African syndrome'. They were peasant immigrants who, with a few exceptions, were not in any way integrated into the French social system. They learnt a few lessons from the French working-class movement (indeed modern Algerian nationalism in a sense originated within the Algerian colony in France), but the Algerian revolutionary ideal only became a real force when it took root among the peasants of Algeria itself.

Even before 1954 the relationship between the Algerians and the police was a very special one, quite unlike that between the police and ordinary criminals – and there was no common language between the two. Any crime surrounded by somewhat unusual circumstances – the rape of a child, for instance – would be automatically put down to the 'North Africans' who were said to 'roam' the district where it occurred. There would be an outcry in the Press and the shanty towns would be searched as a matter of routine. Of course it was true that, like the workers who flocked into the towns from the country in the nineteenth century, the Algerians did constitute what was at that time called 'a dangerous class'. As early as the thirties, the Prefect of Police in Paris had organized a 'North African Squad', just as there was a 'Vice Squad' to deal with pimps. Its methods of action may be judged from the number of its personnel who found their way into the Gestapo.

But there was also a political angle to this repression. On 14 July 1953, as the last of the great traditional processions of the French working class wound its way along the Faubourg Saint Antoine from the Bastille to the Place de la Nation, with a group of Algerians, carrying the Nationalist flag and shouting the slogans of the M.T.L.D. (Messali Hadj's Movement for the Triumph of Democratic Liberties) bringing up the rear, the police opened fire. Six Algerians and one Frenchman were killed; only the Frenchman's death was accidental, yet the trade unions tried to lay at least part of the blame on the Algerians – an eloquent proof of the gulf between the Algerians in France and the rest of the population.

For reasons unrelated to the Algerian problem the Paris police force was completely reorganized when M. Jean Baylot became Prefect of Police. M. Baylot was a Socialist, an ex-prefect of Marseille, and a fanatical anti-Communist. With the support of successive Ministers of the Interior, particularly M. Martinaud-Déplat, he made it his business up to the time of his dismissal by M. Mitterrand in July 1954, to turn the Paris police into a genuine organ of repression, aimed primarily at the Communist Party, but equally capable of dealing with other opponents. Under M. Baylot's régime 'flying squads' were organized, one for each district or suburban area, armed with 'riot sticks' or long wooden batons quite capable of killing a man. At the same time the police began to appear armed with various 'blunt instruments', such as oxhide whips or lead piping. This was a far cry from the good old white batons and the weighted cloaks which were the traditional weapons of the Paris police and had always been thought sufficient to disperse demonstrators.

M. Baylot's system also included secret organizations. At the end of the Indo-Chinese war it was discovered that certain official documents had been lost, and attempts were made to use this case to bring down the Government of M. Mendès-France. As a result the public learned to its astonishment that a special anti-Communist 'network' existed in the Prefecture of Police, under Commissaire Dides, and that M. Dides's principal lieutenant Charles Delarue, was an escaped convict who had been sentenced to twenty years hard labour for working with the Gestapo. This organization had cooked up the most barefaced lies in order to smear any politician who had incurred its displeasure; it even fabricated a 'record' of a meeting of the Central Committee of the Communist Party purporting to show that the Party was getting its information direct from an 'agent', who was none other than the Prime Minister, Pierre Mendès-France! When the case broke Jean Dides was sacked (he later became a Deputy, and later still a member of the Paris Municipal Council), but the Dides network carried on, and still survives today.

It is only a short step from clandestine methods like these to the use of torture. This is not to say that 'scientific' torture was immediately imported into France from Algeria. When the war broke out in Algeria, the F.L.N., which had engineered the insurrection, was practically non-existent in France and the Algerian workers were mainly loyal to Messali Hadj's organization. At first the F.L.N. in France tried to avoid any clash with French authority, and concentrated on the collection of funds to sustain the F.L.N. war effort and on the slow, difficult, and sometimes bloody process of winning over the majority of the Algerian workers in France. F.L.N. operations of a military nature, like attacks on oil installations, did not begin until early August 1958, and then lasted only for a short period.

As far as is known, interrogations using water and electricity tortures first took place in France in September 1957. M. Mairey had just completed his tour as head of the Sûreté; his successor, M. Jean Verdier, was anxious to make it clear that he intended to back up his subordinates, and these subordinates included many police officers who had been brought back from North Africa. In 1958, M. Maurice Papon, ex-Prefect of the Department of

Constantine, became Prefect of Police in Paris. What a police inspector called the 'Algerian-type method' seems first to have been used at police headquarters in the rue Vauban in Lyon.

From 1958 on torture began to supplant traditional police methods in Paris, in the suburbs, and in the provinces, though initially this seems to have been a haphazard rather than a planned development. The most serious instances occurred after some attempted assassinations by Algerians in August 1958. M. André Malraux, the Minister of Information, had said that there would be no more torture. But on 8 September two Paris lawyers, Maître Ould Aoudia and Maître Vergès, drew M. Malraux's attention to two Algerians who had been tortured, one at Argenteuil and the other at Versailles. Both showed obvious marks of torture, and one of them had had to be operated upon for rupture of the spleen. M. Malraux had just proposed that three Nobel prizewinners – François Mauriac, Albert Camus, and Roger Martin du Gard, should visit Algeria to satisfy themselves that torture was no longer being used there. Maîtres Vergès and Ould Aoudia suggested that it was unnecessary to go farther than the prison in Versailles and police headquarters in Argenteuil.

The most important case, however, was that known as the 'Prado' case at Lyon, because it led to a considerable outcry. During October 1958 a number of Algerians were arrested, and their statements implicated three priests belonging to a religious institution responsible for caring for the material and spiritual needs of the Muslims in the Lyon area which was known as the 'Prado Centre'. Two of the priests were charged. Cardinal Gerlier, the Archbishop of Lyon, immediately intervened, stating that the cases brought against his subordinates were false. The statement he made went on:

To support these accusations certain members of the police (I repeat certain members) have gone so far as to force the Muslim accused to sign statements which are clearly false; to obtain this result they have not hesitated to use violence and the gravest cruelties. I feel it is my duty to state that one of those who has been subjected to this treatment is in a serious condition both physically and mentally.

The Minister of the Interior replied by emphasizing that: 'F.L.N. Standing Orders make it obligatory for their members to state in Court that they have been subjected to violence by the police and, as a result, their statements are not valid.' Unfortunately for the Minister's argument, only four of the fourteen Algerians who had been arrested had followed these instructions, but none the less the battle was on. Louis Thomas, an activist working closely with the Military Governor of Lyon (and who was arrested three years later for the murder of an Algerian) accused the Communist Party of 'mobilizing the forces of charity in the service of murder'. The affair ended with a characteristic compromise. The Public Prosecutor, although 'refusing to concede that the awful word torture was justified', publicly admitted that violence had been used against two of the Algerians. He was immediately dismissed. The police stuck to their story that violence had not been used. Cardinal Gerlier made some soothing statements, emphasized his respect for the police, and refrained from publishing the evidence he possessed showing the methods in vogue at police headquarters in the rue Vauban. The charge against the two priests was not pursued. Peace had been restored by a compromise, but at the expense of truth.*

These methods continued to spread, although for many months they enjoyed no legal authority. With the tacit agreement of superior police authority, Algerians were held in police stations well beyond the regulation twenty-four hours after arrest – for what a police officer once termed 'reasons of State'. Very soon, however, it was no longer necessary for the police to break the law. A decree of 7 October 1958 gave them the authority to issue 'confinement orders' in Paris, precisely as in Algiers, and of course the 'place of confinement' was always a police establishment.† Prisoners were thus completely in the power of their

* R. H. Benoit's article in *Esprit*, January 1959, is illuminating on the subject of this affair.

† A similar decree of 24 April 1961 directed against right-wing French extremists authorized the police to keep those arrested 'under observation' for fifteen days. The difference is not merely one of terminology. Those 'under observation' have the right to demand to see a doctor at the end of each twenty-four hours. Very few Algerians were ever placed 'under observation'.

interrogators and could be held until they were 'in a fit state' to be brought before a magistrate.

It was not long before there was a striking illustration of what these 'confinement orders' meant. In December 1959 a group of Algerian students were arrested. They were all placed 'in confinement' in the offices of the D.S.T. in the rue des Saussaies, only a few yards from the Élysée Palace. The majority of them were horribly tortured; in some cases the examining magistrate had to serve the charge on them in hospital. The victims filed complaints and published detailed accounts of their experiences in *La Gangrène*.* The most striking point of these reports is not the barbarity of the methods employed, but the calm self-assurance of the police and their complete confidence in their own immunity. 'The poor old Safeguards Commission!' said one of them; 'every time someone brings a complaint against us the boss promotes us.' *La Gangrène* was suppressed, and M. Debré stated in the Senate that this 'infamous book' had been written by two 'infamous authors in the pay of the Communist Party' and that it was 'a complete fabrication'. But in spite of this the case brought against the publisher was never heard. Other leading politicians, however, apparently reacted somewhat differently from the Prime Minister, and for some time torture was not used in Paris. France was not yet an Algeria. The truth of the reports published in *La Gangrène* was never admitted, but at least the ban on the book was lifted.

But the use of torture is no more than a symptom, though admittedly the worst symptom, of a larger disease. From the summer of 1958 the Algerians in France seemed to be at the mercy of a variety of apparently arbitrary actions by the police. There were 'darkie hunts', when the police fired at sight on any dark-skinned person seen out too late at night; in the autumn of 1958 some Portuguese and Italian workers were shot 'by mistake' during one of these affairs. There were round-ups, as a result of which Algerians were incarcerated for hours or days in sports grounds or other public places. They were then either set free or temporarily interned in the sorting centre which had been set up at Vincennes, one of the gates of Paris; alternatively they might

* Éditions de Minuit, Paris, 1959.

be interned for years in one of the four concentration camps which had been opened in France.* And there were still other police operations, such as that with the charming code-name 'Cosmos', which an Algerian trade unionist described in these words:

The drill is to descend at night on some hotel occupied by Algerians; sub-machine-guns at the ready, the police get everybody up and bring them down into the courtyard or into the street, sometimes still in their pyjamas, even though it may be winter and bitterly cold. They search the hotel, turn everything upside down, and cart five or six suspects off to another hotel at the other end of Paris. There they collect five or six more and take them back to the first hotel. All of them are forbidden to return to their original lodgings. Alternatively they may be carted off to Vincennes and forbidden to reside in the three departments of the Seine.†

The ordinary people of Paris hardly noticed these occurrences and public opinion was only even mildly aroused if, for instance, some 'respectable' citizen was accidently involved, or some young man on his way back from a New Year's Eve party was shot down by a trigger-happy policeman for no reason at all, or some journalist was hit over the head during a demonstration.

But in the first weeks of 1960 a new stage was reached. The *harkis* made their appearance in the Treizième Arrondissement of Paris – in uniform, sub-machine-guns in hand, revolvers at their belts.‡

It soon became known that these *harkis*, who were commanded by French officers and had the status of auxiliary police, were using various forms of violence when interrogating other Algerians in cellars in the Treizième Arrondissement – the ugly word 'torture' was not used at this stage. The numbers of *harkis* increased rapidly. By the beginning of 1961 they were to be seen in all the districts of Paris inhabited by Algerians. The methods

* One of these, that at Saint-Maurice-l'Ardoise in the Var, was for several months used to house O.A.S. supporters. It has now been closed.

† Robert Barrat 'Entretien avec des syndicalistes algériens' ('I Talked to Algerian Trade Unionists'), *Vérité-Liberté*, September–October 1960.

‡ See Paulette Pejus' book, *Les Harkis à Paris 1961* (*The Harkis in Paris 1961*).

they used were various: round-ups, during which they demolished shanty towns and carted off the inhabitants for police checks; individual interrogations, at which the tortures used were at least as brutal as those in vogue in Algeria, even if less refined. A number of eye-witness accounts, including detailed medical testimony did manage to appear in the Press, but they were generally suppressed. Men were being tortured in hundreds, if not thousands; many of them were murdered – and all this was taking place in Paris.

On 18 March 1961 the Prefect of Police, M. Maurice Papon, was summoned before the Paris Municipal Council to give an account of himself. He assumed complete responsibility for the actions of the *harkis* (this is not surprising seeing that he is the author of a book entitled *L'Ère des responsables* – *The Era of Responsibility*) – and he justified their actions in these words:

I was Special Inspector-General [Super-Prefect] in Constantine for two years, from 1956 to 1958. There I learned that the main characteristic of subversive warfare is its secrecy. Clandestine warfare being impossible in a country like ours, where everything ends by being brought into court, I felt that our operations must be shrouded in at least some degree of secrecy.

But what does 'clandestine warfare', or 'secrecy' mean in this context? Any police force is bound to have on its payroll informers who will naturally be recruited from whatever section of the population the police is trying to keep under observation. There were many instances during the Algerian conflict, both in Algeria and France, when active members of the M.N.A. were used as conscious or unconscious agents for this purpose. But it is clear that the *harkis*, who were both armed and in uniform, could not be expected to penetrate F.L.N. cells to break them up from within or provide the police with information. They could only act from outside and by violent methods. In the struggle to 'break' the F.L.N. as the Viet Minh had been 'broken' during the Indo-Chinese war and as the rebels were being 'broken' in Algeria, the *harkis* were intended to be used as the 'bluecaps' were used during the battle of Algiers. The 'clandestine warfare' or 'secrecy' referred to by M. Papon could therefore only be meant to apply to the operations of the French police and also, as M. Papon himself suggests, to the working of the French legal system. The *harkis* worked 'clandestinely' only in the sense that, being subordinate to a police force and a judicial system which were working closely together, they were subject to no official control of any kind, not even the loose form of control which the police and judiciary in Algeria exercised over the forces of repression there.

There was a further advantage in the use of the *harkis*. The affair of *La Gangrène*, the 'Prado' affair at Lyon, and other similar incidents had caused some scandal. In the full limelight of the trial of those accused of an attempt on the life of M. Soustelle, then Minister of Information, one of the men in the dock had recognized in court a police officer who had tortured him. The effect had been disastrous. So, by keeping the task of torturing Algerians in the hands of other Algerians, the police could keep its hands clean.

But those in authority were not merely concerned with the morale of the police. They also had to consider the effect on the outlook of the population of Paris. The Algerian community in Paris formed a ghetto, isolated in its shanty towns and with little contact, even at work, with ordinary Parisians. The fact that the *harkis* were being set loose on the Algerians merely reinforced the racial prejudice never far below the surface in the mental make-up of the people of Paris, and the comforting illusion that 'they are all savages anyway'. It was hoped, not without reason, that the 'man in the street' would let things ride and would be grateful to the police for ridding him of the F.L.N. terrorists who occasionally attacked other Frenchmen, or policemen, in the street and whose stray bullets sometimes caused casualties. This hope proved fairly well founded; but on the other hand 'accidents' sometimes happened. The *harkis* sometimes searched or otherwise molested innocent passers-by, and once even searched the house of a Jewish business man. (Two of them were sentenced for this exploit.) But although the *harkis* soon became unpopular, there were few Frenchmen with the intelligence to link cause and effect.

However, it became increasingly difficult to pretend to Parisians that the war in Algeria, or even that part of it which had over-flowed into France, was no more than a private affair between two sections of the population in Algeria. Plastic-bomb explosions had started in Paris and at the same time four generals had seized power in Algiers. From then on explosions occurred at regular intervals, yet the police did not seem particularly concerned to try and discover the culprits. For a short time, when negotiations had begun, first at Évian then at Lugrin, it looked as if offensive action against the F.L.N. in France in particular, and the Paris Algerians in general, would be reduced if not suspended altogether. At the end of June 1961 the *harkis* were confined to barracks at Fort Romainville, and there was a definite feeling of *detente*.

What happened then? It appears that some senior police officials, who made little effort to hide their sympathy with the O.A.S., deliberately decided to try and force matters beyond the point of no return, and so make it impossible for negotiations to be resumed. Be this as it may, the fact remains that in August M. Michelet who, though not outstanding for his political courage, had always stated that he was a supporter of a peace policy, and had made statements condemning torture, was replaced as Minister of Justice by M. Bernard Chenot. M. Maurice Papon immediately went the rounds of the police stations of Paris and the suburbs assuring the police that they now had authority behind them; police checks at night, 'identity checks', which invariably meant a period in the Vincennes camp, and beat-ups by the *harkis* all began again. Some Algerians had their identity papers removed and in exchange were given passes valid for only twenty-four hours; beatings and 'third degree' once again became an invariable feature of police checks. All this naturally tended to make the Algerians feel themselves outlaws.

The Algerians and the police were now at war. The Algerians began to strike back at the police, sometimes for specific reasons, sometimes apparently at random (sixteen police were killed and forty-five wounded in 1961, most of them in August and September). The reaction of the police was even more savage; dozens of Algerians were thrown into the Seine and others were found hanged in the woods round Paris. The authorities now grew anxious because practically the entire police force was living in a state of unbearable nervous tension. The police unions, to some extent encouraged by their officers, unanimously 'advised' that a curfew should be imposed on the Algerians of Paris, and this was in fact done. An Algerian who for any reason was out after 10 o'clock at night was arrested and sometimes murdered on the spot.

The F.L.N. reply was to organize a vast silent demonstration on the evening of 17 October; 30,000 Algerians marched through Paris, and there were similar processions on each of the next few days. Everything seemed to suggest that the Paris police had on their hands a 'battle of Paris' (M. Maurice Papon's words), and they took advantage of the situation exactly as General Massu's parachute troops had taken advantage of the battle of Algiers. Although the Algerian demonstrators were unarmed, the official police radio gave out that ten policemen had been killed at the Rond-Point de la Défense. In fact there were no police dead. Dozens of Algerians were shot or drowned; more than 10,000 arrests were made; the prisoners were crushed into sports stadia and the Exhibition Park at the Porte de Versailles, where a 'reception committee' welcomed them with blows from pick-hafts, killing many of them. According to police statements quoted by Claude Bourdet in the Municipal Council and not denied, M. Maurice Papon was actually present when dozens of Algerians were killed at police headquarters.

The Government backed up the police to the full; the official figures are obviously false – only two Algerians killed. On 30 October, by which time many accounts had appeared in the Press, M. Claudius Petit, known in the Chamber of Deputies as a man of moderate views, gave a long account of the horrors of 17 October; but the Minister of the Interior, M. Roger Frey, replied that there was not yet even 'a sign of the appearance of a shadow of proof' of the acts of violence of which the Paris police were supposed to have been guilty. The Court of the Department of the Seine gave notice of the opening of some sixty inquiries into murders of Algerians, but no public action of any sort was ever taken against the police murderers – and with good reason.

Worse was to come. It seemed as if the entire population of Paris was in the grip of a wave of racial passion. There was no public outcry either on 17 October or the following days* in spite of the fact that at Orly Algerians were being shipped off in hundreds, theoretically to be returned to their 'native villages' but in fact to imprisonment in the internment camps. The hysterical articles that appeared in certain newspapers were reminiscent of the fear of the nineteenth-century bourgeoisie for the 'savages of the suburbs', or that of the London bourgeoisie of the Chartist demonstrators before the Battle of Peterloo. When the majority in the Paris Municipal Council passed a vote of thanks to the police they were probably doing no more than echo the feelings of the majority of the population; one member of the Council, M. Moscovitch, even advised that the entire Algerian population of France should be sent back to Algeria, and had the audacity to add: 'sinking the boat is not the Municipal Council's job.' The flight of Europeans from Algeria which is still going on as these words are written, underlines the tragic irony of this proposal.

Nevertheless, a reaction eventually set in. Some sections of the police, in particular the General Union of Police Staff Personnel, let it be known by a large majority all this had been none of their doing. A number of condemnatory articles appeared in the Press and the trade unions came out in the same vein, although somewhat late in the day. But nothing could alter the fact that something not far short of a real pogrom had taken place – in Paris – in 1961!†

It will be remembered that one of the by-products of the war in Algeria had been the development of a split right through the repressive organization there. A similar phenomenon now took place in France, though not as a result of the events of 17 October. On 19 December an anti-O.A.S. demonstration occurred in Paris; the police charged and a number of demonstrators were injured. This time the General Union of Police Staff Personnel came out

* One woman was sentenced early in 1962 for insulting the police by shouting 'murderers' from a window overlooking the demonstration on 17 October.

† Immediately after the demonstrations, a group of film technicians, who are members of the Comité Maurice Audin, aided by *Vérité-Liberté*, shot a remarkable documentary film called *Octobre à Paris* which has been banned in France.

openly against M. Papon – the Secretary-General of the Police Union, Monsieur Rouve, the originator of the request for a curfew on the Algerians, was suspended. (He was later dismissed.) In an interview in *L'Express*, M. Rouve publicly accused the head of the Municipal Police, M. Legay, of being an O.A.S. sympathizer. On 8 February 1962, mobile police were again ordered to put down a demonstration which had been organized in protest against a series of O.A.S. attacks. This time eight Parisians were killed, most of them by suffocation in the entrance to the Charonne Métro (Underground) station. The police officer in charge on this occasion had already been accused of having killed an Algerian with his own hands on 17 October.

A crowd of 500,000 Parisians attended the elaborate funeral ceremony for the victims of 8 February. The Government took no action to stop the ceremony and put the blame for these deaths on some imaginary provocateurs who were supposed to have mingled with the demonstrators. In fact it almost seemed as if the Government was seeking support from the demonstrators against its own police, whose action it was no longer capable of controlling.

But how many of the Parisians who processed that day realized that the events of 8 February were no more than a logical sequal to those of 17 October? Only one speaker at the funeral, the representative of the C.F.T.C.*linked the two sets of events. Yet the lesson was clear. A month before the events of 13 May the police had demonstrated in front of the National Assembly, which clearly showed that there was a crisis within the State, and many had come to think that the Paris police would one day be the instrument of a *coup d'état*. The police had not yet reached that point, but they had not been immune to that slow process of debasement of moral standards which springs from open admission of the use of torture and leads to the acceptance of murder as part of the system, which in turn comes from disregarding the rights of the individual and leads to contempt for the authority of the State. But the men who were really responsible for this terrible turn in affairs were not to be found in the ranks of the police.

* Confédération Française de Travailleurs Chrétiens – French Union of Christian Workers.

CHAPTER 8

Confusion in the Judiciary

In January 1962 many Frenchmen suddenly realized that there was 'something wrong with justice' – the head-line of an editorial published on 18 January in *France-Soir*, a newspaper which generally keeps abreast rather than ahead of ordinary French public opinion. Three French officers who had admitted torturing a young Algerian to death had just been acquitted by the Paris Military Tribunal. A few days earlier the word had gone round that on 11 October 1961 (i.e. some time before) three policemen who had admitted using the electrical torture when interrogating four Algerians had been awarded the derisory sentence of a £10 fine by a court at Avesnes-sur-Helpe (department of the Nord) sitting *in camera*. *France-Soir* quoted these examples side by side with some others which at first sight seemed unconnected: for instance, that most of the death sentences passed on F.L.N. members had not been carried out. As if publicly to confirm this impression of confusion, it was announced a few days later, on 25 January, that it had proved impossible to proceed with the trial of a plastic-bomb thrower in the Assize Court at Nîmes because three members of the jury had refused to take the oath, unless forced to do so. They gave various reasons for their refusal, including fear of victimization, but they also stated that the whole case was a political affair which was therefore not their business but the Government's.

Perhaps the jurors of Nîmes were not far wrong. Young Frenchmen, just like young Englishmen and young Americans, are taught that there are three sources of power within the State and that the authority of the judiciary must be kept strictly separate from that of the legislature and the executive. There was a time when, if anybody in Parliament had had the temerity to refer to the magistrates as Civil Servants, he would have been howled down by members of all parties from extreme right to extreme left.

It may well be that this is all just political theory and that in fact the magistrates are entirely dependent on the Government which appoints them, promotes them, and pays them. That is the popular view, and it is often said that the attitude of the judiciary to the problem of torture during the Algerian war has given ample proof that it is true. General de Gaulle is no believer in the theory of separation of powers. On 8 May 1961 he said: 'Strict fulfilment of the tasks which fall to the secular arm of the State, in other words, to the Army, the police, and the judiciary, is both an imperious necessity and a magnificent duty.' He therefore puts a magistrate in the same category as a policeman or a soldier. This might seem reasonable if there was a single well-defined authority within the State, but many cases can be quoted to prove that in France there was at this time more than one State authority and more than one system of justice.

The Algerian authors of *La Gangrène* were arrested in Paris and tortured by the D.S.T. During their interrogation a policeman suggested to one of them that if only he would cooperate he could be taken straight before an examining magistrate, 'my friend Batigne'. There were disquieting connexions between certain judges who had come to specialize in particular types of case and certain sections of the police force – the word 'underground organization' has even been used. When M. Jacques Batigne was one of the examining magistrates at the Court of Paris, he was, curiously enough, the magistrate who dealt with the majority of cases even remotely connected with the D.S.T. – although there are more than a hundred examining magistrates in Paris.*

Perhaps this was only a normal case of specialization – one judge dealing with Algerian affairs while another dealt with fraud, for instance. But this is not sufficient explanation. Take the case of the Algerian already referred to; after describing how he had been tortured, he goes on:

---

* All these problems are dealt with in *Le Bras Séculier* (*The Secular Arm*), published in Paris in 1961 by a magistrate who writes under the pseudonym of Casamayor.

At three o'clock, still hand-cuffed, I was brought before M. Batigne, the examining magistrate. He looked at my twelve days' growth of beard, my swollen face and the scabs on my nose, but merely said, 'You are guilty of an attempt against the security of the State and of reconstituting a banned organization. You are hereby committed to Fresnes prison.' I gazed at him for some time without saying anything. 'What do you want?' he said. I did not reply. Then he said to my guards, 'Take him away.'

The writer of this account, Bechir Boumaza, together with some other Algerians, laid a complaint and an inquiry was opened. The obvious procedure would have been to entrust the inquiry to a magistrate who was clearly impartial. It was in fact entrusted to M. Batigne. However he went through the motions; police officers were summoned and confronted with the plaintiffs, and the director of the Sûreté, who was present, solemnly stated that he supported the police. This was just after *La Gangrène* had been published and suppressed. The examining magistrate went on holiday, came back unexpectedly to Paris for a few hours on 7 August 1959, and signed an order to the effect that no *prima facie* case had been established. France was on holiday by then; those who had been shocked by reading *La Gangrène* were on holiday too.

But the order was difficult to uphold because one of the plaintiffs, Mustapha Francis, had been taken to hospital with a swollen head. The doctor who examined him was satisfied that his symptoms were the result of external injury, but the police had another explanation. They said that Mustapha Francis had mumps! An appeal was made to the court where the order was filed, but the representative of the Public Prosecutor's office again stated that the young Algerian had mumps, saying that the doctor had noted 'puffiness and swelling of the parotid glands and stiffness of the neck, which are the accepted symptoms of this disease, mumps being an inflammation of the parotid gland'. When the case was heard and he was asked for the source of his medical information, he said he had drawn it from the *Petit-Larousse* dictionary, and again demanded that the order should be confirmed. This was done in two stages – in October 1959 in the case of two of the plaintiffs and in March 1962 for the two others

In the first case the grounds for the decision included the following: 'Whereas the Court of Inquiry has heard the only credible witnesses, i.e. the police officers who have been in contact (!) with the plaintiff, and has discovered no new fact to support so serious a charge. . . .'

There were therefore magistrates who were prepared to state in writing that in a case in which an Algerian brought an accusation against the police, only the evidence of the accused was admissible. From what may have been no more than a feeling of solidarity between a magistrate and a policeman or a group of police, a situation had been reached in which the reputation of the whole system was in jeopardy.

Was such an affair typical of the relationship then existing between authority and the judiciary? If justice is to be dispensed in anything like a normal manner, it is essential that the law and the courts should not be trimmed to fit individual cases. But during the Algerian war, and particularly under General de Gaulle's Government, there were striking variations in the relationship between these ingredients in different legal actions.

Laws were made to fit cases, and Parliament was helpless because authority had been delegated to the Executive. A decree of 4 June 1960 did away with the distinction between actions injurious to the internal as against the external security of the State. The latter carried heavier penalties, and the object of the decree was to make Algerians liable to these heavier penalties although they were theoretically French citizens. When the famous 121 intellectuals issued their statement that they 'respected those who refused to bear arms against the people of Algeria and considered that they acted correctly', a new decree was immediately issued, altering the law of incitement to insubordination. When Maître Vergès made an insolent remark in court, the law which lays down that a lawyer cannot be censured during the hearing of a case in which he is taking part was immediately altered. This was no new article of the penal code, but simply an 'anti-Vergès' decree.

There were special tribunals for special cases. Special courts became the order of the day in the French judiciary. A decree

123

of 7 October 1958 laid down that as a general rule military tribunals should be responsible for dealing with members of the F.L.N. and Frenchmen who supported them. After the Generals' *putsch* a 'superior military tribunal' and a 'special military tribunal' were set up to deal with the various leaders of the revolt according to their relative importance. As soon as the superior military tribunal announced that it had found 'extenuating circumstances' in General Salan's case, it was dissolved and replaced by a new military court of justice presided over by a general. At the same time magistrates were made members of purely *administrative* commissions. One magistrate, for instance, was chairman of a commission formed to deal with the administrative detention of men who had not been sentenced by any judicial body.

There were also special trials to fit special cases. Depending on the political situation, one case might be adjourned and another taken, one incident investigated and another allowed to drop. For example, when the leaders of the April 1961 *putsch* were being tried, a semi-official announcement was made that the investigation would be reopened into the affair of the 'one hundred and twenty-one'. It never was, but the announcement served to give an impression of balance and symmetry.

However, trials before the special courts encountered almost insurmountable legal obstacles. Members of the F.L.N. contested the competence of the French Tribunals to try them and their regular Counsel worked out a system to make the legal absurdities of these trials quite clear. On the other side French extremists who were brought to trial asked, not unreasonably, why, if the *coup d'état* of 13 May 1958 was an innocent and lawful affair, the barricades plot of April 1961 and the activities of the O.A.S. should merit the severest repression. During his interrogation Pierre Lagaillarde said sarcastically,

'On 13th May 1958 I was in uniform. I was armed and, as everybody knows, I stormed a public building. So now I turn to the Prosecution and I say to them: the law is the same for all; if I am to be tried for what happened in January 1960, I have a right to demand that I should also be charged for my actions on 13 May, which were much more distinguished!'

The balance between the action taken against the French activists and against the F.L.N. was more apparent than real. The latter were invariably treated as Common Law criminals, whereas the French were treated with the kind of leniency that is given to the politically misguided. The whole course of the 'barricades trial' tended to show Lagaillarde as an impulsive young hero whose heart was in the right place; yet, as a lieutenant in the French Army, he had tortured and murdered with his own hands. But there was no question of bringing this against him, for Counsel for the Prosecution had been legal adviser to General Salan in 1957 and had firmly supported the practice of 'strong-arm interrogations'. At General Salan's trial, Counsel for the Defence, Maître Tixier-Vignancour, did indeed refer to torture but only to the torture which Salan's supporters were supposed to have suffered in 1961. He even dared to make a brief reference to the death of Maurice Audin, certain that no one, not even the President or the Public Prosecutor, would have the courage to remind him that when the battle of Algiers was fought, General Salan was Commander-in-Chief.

These legal absurdities and the practice of passing over awkward facts in silence may represent no more than extreme symptoms of the basic confusion of thought which is the bane of the judiciary in all Western countries today. At the annual meeting of the friends of the review *Esprit* in June 1962, a magistrate had this humorous comment to make:

Justice recognizes three classes of man, the superhuman, which includes officers, policemen, and politicians; human, which includes ordinary members of society and members of the learned professions; and sub-human, which comprises sections of the population which vary according to the circumstances of the time: Arabs, Jews (during the German occupation); the working class; or Communists (during the McCarthy period in the United States).

But the Algerian war exaggerated these distinctions to a degree which was out of all reason. Only by observing this differential treatment of citizens is it possible to see how the French judicial system has worked in the Fifth Republic and how it has faced the problem of torture and the various other injustices which grew out of the Algerian war.

I say French justice, for there was no more justice in Algeria under General de Gaulle than under M. Mollet.* The real problem there was that in the vast majority of cases, there was not even an inquiry. This was especially true of most cases of torture or summary execution carried out by the military or by the police acting on orders. There was hardly a single case of an Intelligence officer or the head of an interrogation centre or a D.O.P. being questioned even as a witness by an examining magistrate. How, for example, could the perpetrators of the massacres of 17 October 1961 have been tried, when they were acting on the orders of their superiors?

In the cases of some men who had committed other crimes, the fact that they had tortured was considered an extenuating circumstance. After the *putsch* of April 1961, Major Rodier, Head of the Intelligence and Operations Centre at Améziane Farm, and his two underlings were arrested as accomplices of the Algiers generals and leaders of the plastic-bomb teams in the department of Constantine. Major Rodier was even transferred to Paris and imprisoned in the Santé Prison. But some secret deal must then have been made, for all three men were quickly released. The authorities were presumably afraid that, if tried, they might make reference to the many other crimes they had committed, and this could have incriminated the whole civil and military hierarchy in Algeria.

In other cases an inquiry was opened, but only with the specific purpose of covering up the truth. For instance immediately after the events of 17 October, the Senate decided, with the agreement of the Minister of the Interior, to set up a Parliamentary Commission of Inquiry. The Public Prosecutor at once countered by announcing the opening of some sixty murder inquiries in the cases of Algerians who had been found drowned or dead in the Paris area. Now, according to French law, a Parliamentary Commission is not empowered to inquire into cases of which the judiciary is already seised. The inquiries never took place, but the Commission could not be set up.

* See Chapter 5. In June 1960 Henri Alleg and his friends were tried by the military tribunal in Algiers. The trial took place in closed court and the accused had to give up any attempt to defend themselves.

A few exceptional cases *were* tried by tribunals in France. Most of these were Algerian cases which had been withdrawn from the local courts 'for reasons of public security'. One or two examples will show how they were dealt with. We have already described how at the beginning of March 1957, the counter-terrorists had set up a private torture establishment in the Villa des Sources in the suburbs of Algiers. The *Écho d'Alger* had noted at the time that even though the interrogation of a 'suspect' might end in his death, the legal authorities were provided with 'interesting information' by this remarkable method. A number of officers, among them Colonel Thomazo and Colonel Fossey-François, were closely associated with the Villa des Sources counter-terrorist group. But it was not until *October 1961* that the case came up for trial, before the Lille military tribunal, which handled it with some reticence and *in camera*. The majority of the accused were of too high a rank to be tried, and were eliminated from the very start: the others had been released on bail. All except one were acquitted, and he was sentenced *in absentia;* on 4 March 1962 he was arrested as an O.A.S. leader. The acquittal had in fact nothing to do with the acts of the individuals on trial. As *Le Monde* pointed out, when it reported the decision of the court, there could be no question of a conviction, for the Army was involved, even though only indirectly.

The perpetrators of the bomb attack on the Casbah of 10 August 1957, which had caused dozens of deaths, were not arraigned before the military tribunal in Lyon until January 1961. The principal accused had already fled, or been set free during the 'barricades' revolt. The remainder were given sentences of three to five years' imprisonment. On three occasions military tribunals in Bordeaux and Paris, sitting in closed court, acquitted military personnel who were guilty of murder and of using torture. There could be no doubt what these verdicts meant. Individuals could not be punished when the crime was that of the administration or the military, and when the only sacrificial lambs that could be offered to the law were those who could not be covered by the mantle of authority.

Finally it is significant that two and only two cases from Algeria were ever referred to a civil judge by the Criminal Division of the

Court of Appeal. The Audin case was referred to a judge in Rennes in April 1959. For some time, the military personnel involved refused to appear before him. One of them, who was summoned, refused to make any reply and stated that if the trial continued, he would throw his medals in the judge's face. The case was nevertheless sent to court, and hung as a continuing threat over the heads of activist officers, who complained bitterly of this during the 'barricades' trial. However, the case virtually came to an end when two witnesses, M. Reliquet, the former Algiers Public Prosecutor, and General Allard stated that the main culprits were to be found within the government of M. Mollet.

The second case, that of Djamila Boupacha, was conducted by a judge in Caen who took his duty seriously, but, at the decisive moment of the case, the Minister of the Armed Forces and the Commander-in-Chief in Algeria both refused to allow the magistrate the documents needed to identify and establish the guilt of the torturers.* Both these cases were stopped after the Évian agreements.†

Thus, during the Algerian war torturers were not brought to justice, either in Algeria or in France. This was not entirely the fault of the judges who awarded the ludicrous sentences to which we have referred. The authorities who allowed cases to drag on for years and who insisted that trials should take place in closed court surely carry a heavier responsibility. In stating openly that torture was a figment of the imagination of the 'enemies of France', they took upon themselves responsibility for these verdicts.

But, although torture was never mentioned in the courts when torturers were in the dock, it was the main issue in the many legal discussions to which the Algerian war gave rise. It was raised by members of the 'F.L.N. supporting networks', not to exonerate but to justify their actions – for they never tried to excuse themselves. At the trial of the Jeanson network, in the presence of the Press, M. Teitgen gave the first public account of his experiences as Secretary-General in charge of the police in

* See *Djamila Boupacha* by Gisèle Halimi and Simone de Beauvoir.
† See Chapter 10.

the Préfecture of Algiers. In December 1961 the publisher of a novel, *Le Déserteur*, which dealt with the problem of desertion from the forces (and had already been suppressed), was charged before a Paris magistrate. The suspected author, who was a deserter, was not present. The publisher of the book, Jérôme Lindon, director of the Éditions de Minuit, called nine witnesses, each of whom had either undergone or been a witness of torture. One of these witnesses, a young professor named Jean le Meur, who had served two years in prison for refusing to take part in repressive operations, made this frightening statement:

'If you convict the man who sounds the fire alarm you cannot convict the fire raiser. If you convict someone who raises his voice against torture you cannot convict the torturer. So if you convict Jérôme Lindon, I say that you are making France a nation of torturers and you will turn the French courts into places which recognize torture as a normal method of investigation.'

The Public Prosecutor smiled and the President of the Court addressed the witness as one might talk to a sick man who must be treated gently.

'You are clearly an extrovert and you obviously have no difficulty in expressing yourself, but it is dangerous to let your tongue run away with you. The Court administers a polite reproof to you for the observations you have just made. I hesitate to use the word ridiculous but your statements verge upon that.'*

The magistrate who used these words was probably quite sincere He obviously saw no connexion between the polite, learned debate over which he was presiding and the horrors which had taken place in Algeria, which was what the witness, who had just returned from the hell of Algeria, was so impudently seeking to establish. Of course it had not, as a general rule, been the magistrates who had used torture 'as a normal method of investigation', but how many of them had refused to make use of the evidence produced by it? The Éditions de Minuit and the author of *Le Déserteur* were fined. When they appealed, the verdict was confirmed. In contrast to other cases, the witnesses at the trial

* The verbatim record of this trial was published in *Provocation à la Désobéissance* (*Invitation to Insubordination*) by Éditions de Minuit, 1962.

of *Le Déserteur* had had a free hearing; but their statements were made more than seven years after the outbreak of the war in Algeria and so could have little influence.

During the first half of 1962 two more cases, one lasting a few days, the other several weeks, kept public interest alive. On 16 January three officers, who had admitted torturing a Muslim woman to death, were acquitted by the Paris military tribunal. On the 23 May ex-General Raoul Salan, the leader of the O.A.S., was allowed extenuating circumstances by the superior Military Tribunal and so escaped the death penalty; this verdict was generally considered to be tantamount to an acquittal. On the face of it there was no similarity between the two cases. One was taken in closed court and we do not know how it was argued. The other was taken in the full glare of publicity with dozens of journalists present – and two firms of publishers have already put out the verbatim record of the trial. In one case the accused were unimportant, colourless personalities; Raoul Salan had been Commander-in-Chief in Algeria and had been referred to by General de Gaulle as his 'loyal servant'. Nevertheless there was a fundamental relationship between the two cases.

On 24 May 1960 a young Muslim woman named Saadia Mebarek was arrested with five of her companions and taken to the operational headquarters of the 9th Zouaves at Fontaine-Fraiche in the suburbs of Algiers. The ostensible reason for her arrest was that she and her companions were suspected of spreading propaganda urging people to abstain at the local elections. She was considered to be the leader of the group. These may be thought peculiar grounds for arrest; for in October 1958 General de Gaulle had laid down in a note to General Salan that there should be freedom of propaganda during the elections and 'freedom of expression for all points of view – I repeat, all points of view'. And during his 'tour of the officers messes' in March 1960 de Gaulle had used the words 'an Algerian Algeria' which were later assumed to mean an independent Algeria.

But repression is a process which works logically. Carrying on propaganda in favour of abstaining was considered to be tantamount to an assumption *a priori* that the elections would not be

free and the candidates would be unrepresentative. It also indicated obedience to the orders of the F.L.N., and probably of the
O.P.A.; and that, as we know, was considered by the military to
be just as dangerous an activity as throwing a bomb. The 9th
Zouaves was not a regiment with an undue proportion of extremists and it had never formed part of the organization which
specialized in repression and torture. Nevertheless the electrical
torture was used on Saadia Mebarek; 'accidents' can always
happen in such circumstances and Saadia Mebarek died. Her
murderers were a regular officer, Lieutenant Maindt, and two
conscript officers, Second-lieutenant Blanié, an engineer in civil
life, and Second-lieutenant Sanchez, a teacher. The girl's body
was dumped in the street, subsequently 'discovered' by a patrol
under the command of Second-lieutenant Sanchez, and taken to
her husband who immediately laid a complaint. There were
usually quick decisions in affairs of this nature, but the three
officers could produce no convincing arguments and there was a
crushing weight of evidence against them. They were accordingly
charged before the military tribunal but were released on bail
while awaiting trial. (It is well known in France that an accused
who has been released on bail is extremely unlikely subsequently
to be sentenced to imprisonment.)

It was no doubt the intention of those dealing with this case –
the Minister for War and his subordinates – to make an example
of these officers and so demonstrate that the State had the power
to punish torturers. Only three days before, the same court had
sentenced Father Robert Davèzies, a French worker-priest, to
three years' imprisonment for having given assistance to the
F.L.N. Moreover, during the Davèzies trial, the President had
cut short those witnesses who referred to the problem of torture,
saying that if and when the court had to deal with a torture case
it would handle it with equal freedom from bias. But though an
example might be made of the accused in the Mebarek case, it
must not be a public example because the morale of the Army,
which was always considered more important than civil morale,
might suffer. So both the Prosecution and the Defence asked that,
as a special measure, the trial should be held *in camera*, to which
the court agreed. There is no means of knowing how the case

went nor what arguments swayed the court and led the military judges to decide in favour of acquittal. The official prosecutor demanded a heavy sentence of solitary confinement. What is clear is that the whole case was little more than a piece of hypocrisy. In the judgement recorded when the Court rose, no mention was made of the articles of the criminal code which forbid torture, hold it to be an aggravating circumstance in the case of any crime, and prescribe the death penalty for it. The three officers were charged with 'inflicting blows and wounds which unintentionally led to death'. So, since any charge of torture had been ruled out of court, there was no case to answer. The three officers had only been doing their duty in arresting the girl. They had interrogated her using the usual methods established by custom; an unfortunate accident had occurred for which they could not seriously be blamed. In short, a banal ending to a commonplace affair.

But the results of this verdict were not quite so banal. The case roused public feeling in circles far wider than those which usually take interest in such matters. A considerable number of men in important official positions, who had hitherto been conspicuous by their silence, signed a petition stating that they were 'convinced that public opinion considers this verdict a scandal'. But this petition and most of the articles written about the case made no effort to link cause and effect, to point out that the acquittal of these three junior officers was merely a single illustration of notorious torturers, both civilian and military, going unpunished. In any case it is doubtful whether French public opinion did consider the decision of the court to be such a scandal. Second-lieutenant Blanié did indeed run into difficulties with the workers in the Grenoble firm where he worked and had to give up his job. Second-lieutenant Sanchez, who was a teacher, went back to his post at Saint-Hippolyte in the Pyrenées-Orientales, but was at once barred from his union and suspended by the board of his school. However, he defended himself, saying to a correspondent of *Le Monde*:

'Back here of course it all looks pretty odd, all these things ... which are supposed to be so morally reprehensible. But out there it's a question of atmosphere ... an atmosphere ... orders ... you know you never get written ones. And I was only conscripted. No one ever mentioned that. One gets into awkward situations . . .'

The population of his village took up the cudgels on his behalf and the words 'we want Sanchez' appeared scribbled on walls.

The case of the three officers had lasted twenty months. Raoul Salan was arrested on 20 April and tried from 17 to 23 May. The facts seemed incontrovertible. On Salan's instructions literally hundreds of men had been murdered by the O.A.S., both before and after the cease-fire. Salan's deputy, General Jouhaud, had been condemned to death only a few days before. Salan did not quibble about details as Jouhaud had done; he admitted his responsibility, made a statement of principle and refused to open his mouth again. It soon became clear that there was an area of common ground – an agreement that nothing that Salan had done before the creation of the O.A.S. and the April 1961 *putsch* was relevant to the case. Both sides paid tribute to the ex-Commander-in-Chief. But although the Algerian war was forbidden territory, the defence scored a clever point by making the O.A.S. appear merely as the logical and inevitable sequel to the battle of Algiers, and the whole of French policy in the war. One of Salan's counsel, Maître Goutermanoff, made the following significant statement:

The entire civilian population of Algeria was drawn together in the struggle against the outlaws. In the country every farmer was an army auxiliary. In the towns there were of course the territorial reserve formations which had been called up to help in the maintenance of order. Then there was the urban security organization – all large towns were divided into quarters, sectors, and blocks; each had its leader and they were all working with the Army. It was their primary duty to report any F.L.N. activity. You can imagine how many there were who had scores to pay off after having been denounced by Europeans, or Frenchmen or Muslims working for France and who as a result had been interrogated or arrested.

Counsel for the defence further commented that in the period just before the Évian agreements the Army was ordered to make a final supreme effort.

Every evening we heard what sounded like victory bulletins on France V. Radio [Radio Algiers], 'so-and-so-many outlaws killed, so-and-so

many prisoners, so-and-so-many F.L.N. arrested'. We said to our-
selves 'these outlaws they're killing, they've got wives and children and
their wives and children are still alive. If in a few weeks we have to
stop fighting we shall have all these wives, all these widows, all these
orphans against us.'

From that moment the fact that there had been killing before
the cease-fire as well as after it, before the April *putsch*, as well as
after it, and that the soldier killers before the *putsch* had been
precisely the same men as the O.A.S. killers after it, ceased to have
any importance. None of the corpses could be laid at the door of
Salan and the whole argument revolved around the political
question: whose was the logical and coherent policy? – that of
Salan, the Republican General, the target in 1957 of a counter-
terrorist organization which contained the first germ of the O.A.S.
(as Maître Tixier-Vignancour agreed with M. Mitterrand, Minister
of Justice at the time) and which appears to have had at least the
tacit support of M. Michel Debré – or that of General de Gaulle,
who had cleverly shifted his ground and was now working for
an independent rather than a French Algeria?

Once the prosecution had failed to produce a counter argument
to the defence case that the only disagreement between General
de Gaulle and General Salan was about means not ends, the court
could not pronounce a death sentence. The public prosecutor's
closing address was an academic lecture in which the words
'death penalty' did not figure.

At the end of Salan's trial the whole of France agreed that the
verdict was a fearful blow for the State. After the acquittal of the
three officers the Minister for War had lodged an appeal 'in the
interests of justice'. After the verdict in the Salan trial it was
decided on ludicrously flimsy grounds to retry the case. In both
cases it was the government which suffered. Which of the two
verdicts was the more serious in its effect? Which of the two
struck more deeply at the roots of an ordered society? It is hard
to say. The effects of judicial decisions are generally neither limited
not unpredictable and when they produce a feeling of revulsion,
that feeling generally reflects the attitude of mind of a whole
nation.

CHAPTER 9

Confusion in the Nation

THE ordinary citizen is usually protected from violence by his Government, in the widest sense of the word. In normal times very few people come into actual contact with violence in its quintessential form, torture. In his admirable book *Les Damnés de la terre*, Frantz Fanon, who was both a psychiatrist and an anti-colonialist philosopher, describes the psychological turmoil into which torture plunges both torturer and tortured. He tells of a policeman who conscientiously carried on with his job of torturing for eight hours a day and who came to consult Fanon as a psychiatrist because he had reached the stage where he could no longer differentiate between his professional and his family life so that he was continually tempted to torture his wife and children. Both France and Algeria have now been scenes of violence for more than seven years; for Algeria the consequences will certainly be serious, for it is not easy to re-integrate a terrorist into normal society. But the problems may well be solved because an entirely new society and an entirely new state will have to be constructed there. But what of France?

A whole machine of deception has been built up, which reaches from the police officer who uses torture, via the judge who accepts the results of the interrogation as valid evidence, to the Prime Minister who either issues a denial or says nothing. More important still, a whole cross-section of the youth of the nation has been brought violently face to face with problems for which it was mentally almost entirely unprepared.

There was indeed nothing that could possibly have prepared the youth of France for the situation which it was to encounter during the war in Algeria. No proper preliminary instruction had been given, either by the political parties, by the trade unions, or by the church. When the reservists were recalled in 1955–6, the problem of torture was entirely unknown to public opinion. The young Frenchman went off to Algeria with his ears full of slogans and his head full of false ideas. Some thought that they were going to what was merely another bit of France; others thought that the only obstacle to agreement between the French and the Algerians was a handful of rich settlers. These boys were staggered to discover that there were whole quarters in Algiers and Oran which were entirely European and to find themselves being urged by the lower-class French Algerians to use methods of action which would produce quick results. War carried out on mountain paths and in alleyways was a terrible experience for those involved in it. Their enemy was invisible, the population was silent and hostile; the sight of the mutilated bodies of men they had known led to reprisals. Yet in another sense life was easy in a conquered country and even the worst excesses seemed to have the blessing of their commanders.

As the young Frenchman stepped into Algeria he was immediately caught up in two close-knit webs: colonial society and the Army. 'Psychological action' did not convince many Muslims, but its advocates succeeded in convincing both themselves and many of those under them. It was an astonishing business, in many ways reminiscent of the 'double-think' of George Orwell. The young Frenchman was not there to make war but supposedly to 'pacify', and pacification proved to be worse than war; he was supposed to be the protector of Muslims terrorized by the rebels, yet he found himself surrounding villages with barbed wire and card-indexing the inhabitants; he was supposed, in President Coty's words, to be the representative of 'French generosity', yet he found himself torturing or putting to death defenceless prisoners. His Catholic faith had taught him that torture was a crime, and he was occasionally reminded of this by some Army chaplain, but he found that there were other priests who justified the use of torture and he watched the Archbishop of Paris solemnly administering the sacrament to General Massu. If he was a worker and a Marxist, he was at a loss to know how to treat the *fellaghas* (rebels), who appeared to have so little in common with his imaginary picture of revolutionaries of the nineteenth century.

All this of course applies primarily to the early years of the war. From 1958 onwards the church and the political parties did try to lay down rules of conduct for young soldiers, and in some extreme situations these rules were of value. Energetic members of the youth associations played an important part in the conscript element's refusal to take part in the *putsch* of 22 April which led to its failure. But they could do little to help in preparing these same young men to face the problem of torture.

I must at this point quote a document which will show better than any theoretical arguments how a man can turn into a murderer and dream up for himself attractive but senseless arguments to justify his actions. It is a young soldier's letter published in 1958 by the worker priests of the 'French Mission'. It reads:

They used to ask for volunteers to finish off the guys who had been tortured (there are no marks left that way and so no danger of a witch-hunt later). I didn't like the idea – you know how it is – shooting a chap a hundred yards off in battle – that's nothing, because the guy's some way off and you can hardly see him. And anyway he's armed and can either shoot back or buzz off. But finishing off a defenceless guy just like that – No! Anyway I never volunteered and so in the end I was the only one in the whole sector who had never finished off 'his' guy. I was called 'chicken'. One day the captain called me out and said: 'I don't like having chickens around – get on with it, the next one's yours.' Well, a few days later there were eight prisoners who had been tortured and who had to be finished off. They called me and in front of all the boys they said: 'He's yours, chicken, get on with it.' I went up to the guy. He looked at me. I can see his eyes looking at me now. The whole thing revolted me. I fired. The other chaps finished off the rest. After that it wasn't so bad, but the first time – I tell you that turned me up. It's a nasty business I know, but when you think about it, all those guys are criminals really, and if you let them live they'd only go on killing old men, and women and children. You can't let them carry on like that. So really we're ridding the country of all that scum. And then they're really all pro-Communists, these guys. Do you see now?

It may be argued that this is only an individual case, but it is exactly like a large number of others. Jean Carta, a left-wing intellectual on the staff of *Témoignage chrétien*, tells a frightening story in 'L'Engrenage' ('Caught in the Machine').* As a lieutenant in the Army he had, after some hesitation, arrested a villager

* *Vérité-Liberté*, July–August 1960.

because he had no identity card. He handed him over to a gen-darme, who quite casually, and as a matter of routine, tortured him. The story ends:

A week went by and then I used to see my young victim quite often. I had him looked after by the medical orderly. There are thousands of cases like his but this one got on my conscience. I didn't try to make excuses for myself, for no excuses were possible; but I did at least try to explain to him that I hadn't meant it to happen. He looked at me with his red-rimmed eyes. There was no hostility in them, just in-difference. I would rather that he had blazed at me than just looked at me with those eyes, which spoke of so much suffering caused by the wickedness and beastliness of men – men from France.

Such stories leave their mark. But we must not generalize too much about what the war in Algeria meant to the young Frenchman. Many of them hardly ever left their barracks in Algiers or Oran, at least until the tragic events following the proclamation of the cease-fire. There were also the officers and men of the S.A.S. who devoted themselves to a sort of high-powered Boy Scout movement and who came back from Algeria with a perfectly clear conscience. Then again there were the troops of the specialized formations, particularly the parachute troops, who had to fight hard and almost in-cessantly, and who were completely brutalized by the life they led. They raced from one end of Algeria to the other without meeting a soul, as if they were operating in the desert. They knew nothing of the country in which they were fighting, nor of the men whom they fought and sometimes tortured. They had lost all individual and collective feeling other than a sort of gang loyalty. One of them, Pierre Leulliette, in *Saint-Michel et le dragon*,* the book which he wrote in order to get out of the Army, said: 'We were like a pack of wolves.'

I happened to meet one of these men once on a journey. It was September 1961 and he had just come out of military detention in Germany where he had been serving a sentence for acting as bodyguard to General Challe during the April *putsch*. With vivid gestures he told how, during the *putsch*, he and his fellow paratroopers had mown down a crowd of 2,000 to 3,000 Muslims

* Shortly to be published in English by Heinemann.

with machine-guns. There was not a word of truth in it, and nothing of the sort had in fact taken place. But it was 'his' dream and he stuck to it and went back over it with morbid self-satisfaction. In the dining-car where we were sitting, two rich-looking business men politely tried to explain to him that the duty of the Army was to obey the civil power, but any such idea was obviously far above his head.

Apart from such individual cases can any reasonable estimate be made of the proportion of the youth of France which found itself confronted by this problem? In November 1960 *La Vie catholique*, a popular magazine with a large circulation, published a questionnaire for its readers who had served in Algeria. It received several hundred detailed replies from readers of every social level and every shade of opinion.* Among other things the questionnaire asked what had been the reader's worst experience; 126 replies referred to the hardships of the war as such; eighty-seven referred to a scene of torture which the reader either knew about, had heard about, had seen, or in a few cases had taken part in; forty-five referred to atrocities committed by Frenchmen during the repression; 104 did not reply or preferred not to reply; only six referred to their own wounds; and five said simply 'my time in Algeria'. These figures are probably not representative of the entire 'youth of the *djebel*', but they do prove that we are dealing with much more than individual cases and that the numbers involved show that the question of how the youth of France reacted when faced with the problem of torture is a real one.

Let us now try to define more exactly how they did react. The majority of young Frenchmen seem to have accepted the scenes which they were forced to witness fairly calmly, though this does not mean that they suffered no long-term effects. To *La Vie catholique*'s question 'Do you often think about Algeria?' 476 young people replied that they thought about it a great deal (some said 'every day – at night too – it is becoming an obsession'); 115 thought about it 'a bit'; and eleven 'not at all'.

A minority returned from Algeria as complete perverts. Today they are members of the O.A.S. commandos and the criminal

* Xavier Grall, *La Génération du djebel*, 1962.

gangs to be found in the cities of France. Among this minority are the ex-paratroopers who appear before the assize courts and plead that they have been taught to kill. The problem of youth is today a critical one in all industrialized countries, but there can be no doubt that the war in Algeria and the practice of torture must bear some responsibility for the fact that it is so much more serious in France.

Another minority resisted while serving in Algeria, only to find themselves in prison for refusing to take part in repressive operations. One of these, a reserve officer and a teacher called Jean le Meur, wrote: 'Even if one has a cushy job, even if one is merely in an office, one is part of the machine of repression; one is part of the organization and so in some measure responsible for what it does.' The nature of the war in Algeria also led to a number of similar incidents in France itself, in which young men preferred the risks of mutiny or desertion to joining the war. A few even deserted in Algeria; for instance Noël Favrelière, a sergeant in a parachute unit, refused to be involved in the execution of a prisoner, set the prisoner free, and then went into the maquis and so to Tunisia.*

On their return to France many of the young soldiers and even more of the older ones, for example those who had been students and had had their call-up postponed and those who had been recalled by the Faure and Mollet governments although they had already taken up a profession, were determined to get the record straight. Many of them published accounts of what they had seen and helped to launch a propaganda campaign against the war in Algeria and the methods employed there. Particularly after 1958, many of them became members of clandestine organizations with the object of supporting the F.L.N. or inciting men to desert. One of them, Jean-Claude Paubert, a member of the 'Jeanson network', made the following statement at his trial:

I was in Algeria in 1956. I was an active left-wing supporter; both before and after being put into uniform I protested against being sent to Algeria. I finally agreed because I considered that it was my duty to go there in order to protect and help those Frenchmen who were stuck there. At the gendarmerie at Letourneux soldiers in French

* See his book *Le Désert à l'aube*, 1960.

uniform forced Algerians under threat of torture to have intercourse with dogs. After this I began to think about the problem of Algeria and I came to see that ordinary people are wrong to be continually fulminating against torture; for under a colonial régime torture is legal; it is a fundamental and legal attribute of a régime of oppression.

Whatever one may feel about such a statement it clearly raises questions of both fact and morality. Factually, was any real protest ever raised in France against the practice of torture? The answer is not as easy as it might seem. Hundreds of eye-witness accounts were published in France, some of which achieved enormous publicity; for instance, 66,000 copies of Henri Alleg's *La Question* were sold before it was suppressed and after its suppression a further 90,000 copies of a semi-clandestine edition were passed round by hand. Accounts and articles appeared only occasionally at first, and in 1956, when the public as a whole was broadly in favour of the policy of the Government of M. Mollet, there were hardly any. When the reservists began to return from Algeria in the spring of 1957 a number of accounts again appeared, somewhat tentative at first, but later more and more outspoken. At that time some of the writers who denounced torture, such as Pierre-Henri Simon, who brought out a pamphlet entitled 'Contre la torture' in March 1957, felt that a distinction could be drawn between the practice of torture and the conduct of the war in Algeria. But this distinction was not tenable for long and those who denounced torture soon became unanimous in calling for negotiations and peace. All the newspapers from the left centre to the extreme left, i.e. from *Le Monde* to *L'Humanité* (the mouthpiece of the Communist Party), and including *L'Express*, *France-Observateur*, and *Le Canard enchaîné*, took part in the campaign (except those controlled by the Socialist Party), as did the small left-wing parties and the Communists. In short no country involved in similar horrors has ever permitted publication of such complete documentation on the subject – a decisive proof of the difference between France and Nazi Germany.

But we must look somewhat deeper. It was the not usual organized groups which led the campaign, but individuals or small groups. Although Henri Alleg was a Communist, his testimony was not published by the Communist Party Press, but by Éditions de Minuit, which, although originally a clandestine press founded during the German Occupation, had subsequently become a perfectly normal publishing house specializing in literature and with no great interest in politics. Paradoxically it was an article by a right-wing journalist, André Frossard, in an ultra-right-wing newspaper, *L'Aurore*, which first made the scandal of Djamila Bouhired a public issue – three weeks after the publication of a little book on the subject which had been almost universally ignored. It was *Le Monde* which published the most important official documents on repression, and more especially the reports of the 'safeguards commission' and the International Red Cross. The political parties were in the main far less vigorous. Some, like the Socialist Party and the Radical Party, were themselves involved up to the hilt in the policy of repression, so their members could not express their views freely until the parties had split. The Communist Party had actually voted in favour of the 'special powers' in 1956, in order not to break with the Socialists who were then in power. In any case, its attitude at the time of the Hungarian Revolution and its continuous support for Stalinism made many of its protests suspect. Like some of the other parties it had too many skeletons in its own cupboard.

The anti-torture campaign was primarily organized by the intellectuals, including the intellectuals of the Communist Party, who loudly criticized their party's attitude. Professor Capitant's gesture in breaking off his course of lectures when the 'suicide' of his ex-pupil, Ali Boumendjel, was announced caused a considerable stir. On 2 December 1957 the Science Faculty of Paris insisted, against the 'advice' of the Minister of Education, on accepting Maurice Audin's doctoral thesis, although he had 'disappeared' on 21 June 1957. His colleagues then organized a 'Maurice Audin Committee' which, though including men of all shades of political opinion, was entirely independent of any political party, and soon became an independent organization for anti-torture propaganda, fulfilling two functions: first that of a pressure-group on the authorities and on the Press, which it fed with information and opinions; secondly that of an information centre for its members, who included literally thousands of members of the teaching profession in Paris and the provinces.

The Audin Committee is only one example among many. A whole vigorous independent left-wing movement appeared, unconnected with the old political parties and at times in opposition to them. It even had its own Press, since the normal Press was frequently subject to suppression by the government. In January 1958 a paper entitled *Témoignages et documents* (*Documents and Eye-witness Accounts*) appeared with the avowed object of reprinting regularly all the articles suppressed by the Government and distributing them by any method that came to hand. In May 1960 a second paper, *Vérité-Liberté* (*Truth and Liberty*) was launched, working on the same lines but, in addition to counteracting official censorship, publishing material which the major newspapers could not or would not carry. Of course these publications catered principally for the more vigilant and vocal section of the public, but they were nevertheless significant as an indication that the spirit of protest was still alive.

Some of those who were carrying on the campaign against torture went further. In May 1957 the philosopher Francis Jeanson, who was later to become the leader of an organization supporting the F.L.N., published an article in *Esprit* on the death of his friend Ali Boumendjel in which the concluding paragraph read:

The case of Ali Boumendjel may have aroused much of French public opinion to what is happening, but it is only one case among thousands of others. The truth is only just beginning to emerge, but I would like to emphasize here the terrible danger which France, and particularly the French youth, is running. If it should prove quite impossible to get our successive Governments to follow a healthier policy, those who continue to believe in the moral values which they have been taught may be increasingly tempted to side with the victims of France against the France to which they belong. This was the question I faced when I learnt of the death of Ali, who was my friend. Must the French people be condemned for the second time in fifteen years to carry on treason against the legal government of France?

Our next question must be 'Did the anti-torture campaign, which had so profound an influence in intellectual circles, ever become a significant factor in politics, or in any way stir the conscience of the country?' Here again there is no simple answer.

In Algeria those officers who felt that in torturing they were doing their duty and carrying out the orders of their government, were of course exasperated by the campaign. One of them, Philippe Héduy wrote:

Here, if we put a prisoner on the magneto, and get information which prevents some vehicle carrying ten people being blown up, everybody turns a blind eye, because there is no other way of operating. But at home there's always someone who finds out, charges to the defence of the murderers, and calls us torturers.*

Héduy was a typical representative of the young right-wing movement which was a product of the Algerian war. He was responsible for this impassioned appeal in a paper with O.A.S. leanings:

You will be made to pay, all you academics. You will pay for lecturing us, calling us murderers, for all your meetings and the motions you pass, and the lies you spread around. You will pay for the martyrs you make and for the deaths for which you are responsible. You will pay for your vile anti-torture campaign because it attacks the honour of the Army and anything which does that shall cost you dear. You academics have slung so much mud at us that you have got your own hands dirty; you have become what you yourselves would call 'irredeemables'.

Officers who were attacked felt that the government was not acting with sufficient energy against the instigators of the campaign and so they too turned against the authorities, in spite of the reassuring statements which the latter issued. Important witnesses at the 'barricades' trial, like General Massu and Colonel Godard, expatiated upon the exasperation felt in the Army at the end of 1959 and beginning of 1960 when documents on the Audin affair were published in France.

It seems unlikely that the anti-torture campaign saved any lives in Algeria. On the contrary, there was a sinister inverted development. The further the war in Algeria went, the more summary execution rather than mere torture seemed to become the rule; for there was no danger of the victims of summary execution talking later. But the vigour of the anti-torture campaign does seem to have made some impression on the Algerians and may

* *Au Lieutenant des Taglaïts*, 1961.

perhaps be a factor in an eventual reconciliation of the two countries.

However, it is France not Algeria we must examine. On 9 March 1958 Abu produced a frightening cartoon in the *Observer* showing the French Prime Minister, M. Félix Gaillard, pointing with one hand to a man with his hands tied behind his back, labelled 'French opposition Press', and with the other to another man with his hands tied behind a deeply scarred back, labelled 'Algerian suspect'. From an electric point in the ceiling hung a long wire ending with two clip-type electrodes. The caption read 'If only HE would talk and YOU would shut up'. But again the situation was not as simple as this. The individuals and the newspapers who published the first incontrovertible proofs of the methods being used in Algeria undoubtedly thought that they would immediately raise an enormous outcry. Many thought back to the Dreyfus affair, but they were forgetting how many years elapsed between the moment when all thinking people were convinced that the little Jewish captain was innocent and the moment when he was officially and publicly reinstated. They forgot too that the circumstances now were fundamentally different and that Dreyfus was not a colonial subject. Nevertheless the historical analogy seemed so apt that many expected legal actions with public arguments and counter-arguments which would cut through the emotional aspects of the problem and gradually get at the truth.

In the event the public debate which took place was of a very different nature. Very soon the campaign *against* torture was countered by a campaign *in favour of* torture, less highly organized but perhaps for that very reason more effective. A typical story told by that brilliant assayist, Alfred Fabre-Luce, may serve as an example:

The civil Inspector-General [super-prefect] on special duty in Oran was visited by a member of the Commission for the Safeguarding of Individual Rights. He asked him into his office, sat down at his desk, and said, 'We have just captured a terrorist, bomb in hand. We are convinced that he knows, but will not tell us, the names of thirty other terrorists, each of whom is preparing to throw a bomb. We can either put him through an unpleasant quarter of an hour or risk the lives of

145

some 300 innocent human beings. Which shall we do? Put yourself in my place and decide'. The visitor stammered, 'Well ... I think ... it might be better. ...' The Inspector-General cut him short. 'You need not worry, the decision was taken three months ago. The citizens of Oran were able to sleep in peace.'

Volumes have been written to explain and justify the use of torture. They range from theoretical treatises, like Colonel Trinquier's, to popular novels. In February 1957 an evening newspaper published a full-scale inquiry by a journalist and ex-paratrooper, Jean Lartéguy, which set out to prove that the accusations made against his fellow-paratroopers in connexion with the Djamila Bouhired affair were fabrications. In 1960 the same author published the first volume of an epic of the paratroopers, in which the practice of torture is described and fully justified. His books had an enormous sale, far larger even than that of Henri Alleg's *La Question*. In other novels, like those of Cécil Saint-Laurent, a specialist in cheap eroticism, torture is depicted as almost a pleasant affair. One such novel describes the water torture of a girl in a well-fitted bathroom by officers so courteous and polite that they do not ask her to remove her slip. As soon as she has talked, her torturers sit her on a soft pile carpet and put a bathing wrap around her to get her warm again. This kind of novel naturally also has a love-interest, which is often concerned with a lovely young Muslim girl's passion for the paratrooper who has tortured her. But these are books which make some sort of pretence to being literature. Alongside them are the cheap spy novels, sold in their millions, in which the hero is a French Secret Serviceman who gets the better of his opponents by using the worst forms of violence against them.

This is perhaps not the most serious aspect of the affair. More important is the silence of the big newspapers, radio and television. The Audin case was the one which created the greatest stir in France; the left-wing Press even saw it as a new Dreyfus affair. Yet during the two days of December 1959 which followed the publication by the Maurice Audin Committee of a detailed account of the death of the young Algiers professor, of the ten morning and evening Paris dailies with a total circulation of 4,050,000 copies, the four largest (with a combined circulation of 3,140,000) devoted no more than eighty-three lines to it; and of these only twenty-one dealt with the case for the Prosecution whereas the remaining sixty-two were devoted to the Government reply. A story which *Le Monde* had thought worth a leading article was not even mentioned in some of the other daily newspapers. Few Frenchmen read more than one newspaper, and when they do, readers of a moderate daily will automatically assume that what appears in the Communist Press is false (and vice versa). But the majority will simply know nothing about it. So, although all those who really *wanted* to know were well-informed, the majority of Frenchmen knew nothing, or believed that all accusations against the Army must be the work of scoundrels who invented their stories in order to distract attention from F.L.N. atrocities.

After October 1961, stories began to circulate about violence being used against adherents of the O.A.S., and it was then the turn of the right-wing Press to launch an anti-torture campaign, producing some remarkable about-turns. Proven torturers published articles indignantly condemning torture. The majority of the left-wing Press preserved a discreet silence, but, to the astonishment of the new school of protesters, *Le Monde* and the Maurice Audin Committee continued to remonstrate vigorously against any use of torture.

Such then was the general atmosphere in which the anti-torture campaign was conducted – with negligible results. There were one or two fortunate occasions when the silence was broken and words gave place to action. A notable example was in the late summer and early autumn of 1960. The Melun talks had broken down at the end of June; on 5 September, General de Gaulle gave a Press Conference at which he appeared to lay down unacceptable conditions for the resumption of negotiations; the following day the trial of the Jeanson Network opened and continued until 3 October. The background to the acts of the accused was complex but it gave those, like Jean-Paul Sartre, and others who felt the systematic use of torture to be a scandal, a platform from which to publicize their horror. On 6 September, in a 'Declaration on the Right of Insubordination in the War in

Algeria' the 121 intellectuals stated, among other things: 'Must we recall that, fifteen years after the destruction of Hitlerism, French militarism has now reached the stage where, as a result of the requirements of this war, it is re-introducing the practice of torture and making it once more an institution in Europe?' The anti-torture campaign had prepared the ground for this declaration, and the action the Government took against its signatories only increased its very considerable impact. In the words of *Life* magazine, 'moral barricades' were being raised against the Government. In the course of a few weeks the political climate changed fundamentally. The trade unions and the left-wing political parties came out openly with statements on the crisis of conscience gripping the youth of the country. The Government Party, the U.N.R. (Union for New Republic), found itself unable to agree upon a resolution censuring the action of the '121' and the 'scandal of the Jeanson trial', because its Muslim members refused to deny the truth of the statements about the systematic use of torture made at the trial by men like M. Teitgen. For the first time since 1956 the left-wing came out into the streets. On 5 October, the National Association of French Students stated, *'The youth of France will not be able to hold up its head in the national community* unless all those who are on the side of peace by negotiation give open expression of their determination to bring this conflict to an end.' This meant that a Union representing more than 100,000 students was prepared to state publicly that the solidarity of the nation was threatened by torture being an essential element in the war. On 27 October, several hundred thousand people throughout France demonstrated in the streets.

It is of course doubtful whether all those who demonstrated realized the vital problems which the use of torture raised, but the students at least were now convinced. On 23 April 1961, during the generals' *putsch*, and just after the night when Paris had lain under threat of attack by the parachute troops, there was a spontaneous demonstration by several thousand students shouting not only anti-Fascist slogans but also 'justice for Audin'. The majority of the teaching profession was deeply disturbed. But other sections of society were, in general, still indifferent. Most of the daily papers read by the Paris workers had been completely silent about both torture and the crimes of the O.A.S. In any case, it is harder for the working class than for students or teachers to express their feelings on a subject like torture.

Although the general public in France had gradually come to feel disgust for the war in Algeria in general and the methods employed in particular, it was not the anti-torture campaign which ended the war. The decisive factors were General de Gaulle's policy, war weariness, the pressure of international opinion, and, most important of all, the continued resistance of the Algerians. The demonstrations of October 1960 did less to convince the French people than the demonstrations by the Algerians in December 1960 and on 17 October 1961. Nevertheless, the campaign against torture had raised problems far wider than the Algerian question. It was not the police, nor even the Army, which was in the dock. It was the State itself, in its capacity as the guiding force of modern society.

Because of this, the problem of torture was not solved by the end of the Algerian drama. Even the authorities realized this. On 1 February 1962, the Minister for War found it necessary to send to Commanders-in-Chief at home and overseas a circular expressing anxiety at 'the increasing loss of a sense of responsibility and lack of respect for human dignity on the part of certain officers and N.C.O.s who are prepared to use physical violence on recruits'. There is no reference to Muslim terrorists in this document and it is hard to see what 'information' an N.C.O. could get by torturing a young soldier – for that is what was happening. In September 1961, the review, *Esprit*, published an article with the resurrected title 'La Gangrène' giving a frightening account of the brutalities inflicted on a young French soldier in Germany because for some trivial reason he had incurred his sergeant-major's displeasure. (At the request of the Minister for War, this edition of *Esprit* was suppressed, the first time such a thing had happened in the history of the review.) Cruelties of this sort are not unknown in any army. In *corps d'élite*, like the American Marines and the French parachute troops, they are often considered part of the process of initiating a recruit to the manly qualities of the military profession. But in the light of the

Algerian drama no one can deny that our civilization will be judged by the number of problems of this nature which it throws up and the answers it contrives to find to them.

CHAPTER 10

The Prospect for the Future

THERE is a well-known passage of Thucydides dealing with the state of public morality in Greece during the Peloponnesian War just after the Corcyra massacre. It says:

To fit in with the change of events, words, too, had to change their usual meanings. What used to be described as a thoughtless act of aggression was now regarded as the courage one would expect to find in a party member; to think of the future and wait was merely another way of saying one was a coward; any idea of moderation was just an attempt to disguise one's unmanly character; ability to understand a question from all sides meant that one was totally unfitted for action; frenzied violence came to be considered an attribute of a real man.*

A similar misuse of words has become characteristic in France today. Even the executioners themselves do not have the courage to call a spade a spade. Torture became 'strong-arm interrogation'. Colonel Trinquier, for instance, never said, 'This suspect is to be tortured'; he would say,

In this case, interrogation will take place without the presence of a legal representative. If the suspect makes no difficulty about giving the information required, the interrogation will be over quickly, otherwise specialists must use all means available to drag his secret out of him. Like a soldier he must then face suffering and perhaps even the death which he has so far avoided.†

The torturers also had their special jargon. An officer who had been in the Army in Algeria observed: 'The electric torture is called rock 'n' roll and the water torture underwater breast-stroke.'‡ France has sometimes been very close to the situation described by Thucydides. Some Air Force officer cadets once had

* Thucydides, *The Peloponnesian War*, Book 3, published in the Penguin Classics, 1954.
† *La Guerre moderne*.   ‡ Jean Carta, *Esprit*, May 1958.

to write an essay on the following passage in Amiel: 'Those who sigh for justice merely show that they are unhealthily oversensitive. One must be able to do without justice; a real man must be independent of it.'

The first point in the programme of any movement aiming to restore France (or almost any other country) to health would have to be the re-establishment of the true meaning of words. All too often words were used as a screen between the hideous realities of the Villa Susini or the El-Biar sorting centre and the complacency of the ordinary French citizen. The Frenchman heard of violence, of cruelty, and of torture, but how could he picture what M. Teitgen called the 'witness cringing in the dark', tied down naked on a plank and surrounded by his torturers laughing at him?

Just after the end of the Algerian war there was a vitally important moment when the truth was for once uttered and words given their true meaning. It was on 1 August 1962 (when France was again, of course, on holiday), during the trial of three deserters, two officers, and one N.C.O., all O.A.S. members charged with a murder committed in Paris. Captain Estoup, an ex-officer of the 1st Foreign Legion Parachute Regiment, who had taken part in the *putsch* of 22 April, had the courage to say, loudly and clearly, what General Allard had said in muted tones and polite phraseology to the examining magistrate in the Audin case. Captain Estoup asked the Judges of the military court of justice set up by General de Gaulle after the Salan trial:

'How can it happen that a brilliant young St Cyr* cadet, one of the outstanding young men of his intake at the Military Academy – how can it happen that this young man, a second-Lieutenant in 1955, today stands accused before a military court? What has happened? Who is responsible for this situation? Who can explain why, for the past year, so many officers and sometimes N.C.O.s have been on trial, all, or nearly all, of whom served in the same type of formation – parachute troops, Foreign Legion, or commandos? My answer is only a partial answer but it is bitter and pregnant.

'In conventional warfare the more difficult operations, like taking a fort or mopping up a trench, are usually entrusted to *élite* formations,

* St Cyr is comparable to Sandhurst or West Point.

sometimes called "special" formations. In a war like the Algerian war too the more difficult operations were entrusted to formations sometimes called "*élite*", sometimes "special", but more often "operational". It was their job, where necessary, to rout out the rebels from their most inaccessible hide-outs; but, more important, it was also usually their job to build up the Intelligence dossiers. The reason why the officers and N.C.O.s, who have been before military courts in the last year, all come from these formations is that they were all at some time ordered to collect intelligence and to do so "by all means available". Mr President, in military language the phrase is "to gather intelligence", in polite language it is "to push an interrogation", in French it is "to torture". I hereby state on oath, and no one can contradict me, that Lieutenant Godot [one of the accused for whose defence Captain Estoup was a witness], like hundreds of his fellow-officers, was ordered to get information by the use of torture. I know neither the rank nor the name of the overall commander who gave this order, and you will find no written copy of it. But I do know that, as far as the 10th Parachute Division was concerned, it was on General Massu's instructions that this order was distributed to the operational level. If you tell me that all this is a pack of lies, I shall ask you how it was that on a single night in January 1957 four regiments of the same division simultaneously began to "collect intelligence" in Algiers. And if no order was issued for this operation, how did it get a code-name? It was called "Champagne".

'I do not know what sort of mental turmoil someone who gives an order like this must go through; but I do know the sense of shock and revulsion suffered by those who have to carry it out. All the fine ideas and the illusions of the young St Cyr cadet crumble into nothing when he comes face to face with this stranger out of whom he is ordered to drag information. He is like a young curate whose vicar has gone mad and ordered him to rape the ladies of his parish because they seem to be hesitant or lukewarm in their religious convictions.

'But you will say: "Then why did not the young St Cyr cadet refuse to carry out the order?" Because the ultimate end had been so described to him that it appeared to justify the means. It had been proved to him that the outcome of the battle depended on the information he obtained, that the victory of France was at stake. He was caught in the toils of a monster whose ethics prescribed that "the end justifies the means". It was a crusade and in every age crusades have had the same characteristics.

'If the means are justified only by the end, there is no justification at all unless the end is achieved. If it is not, nothing is left but a senseless pattern of dirty indelible stains. The fact that there was such a high proportion of "out-and-outers" in the operational units did not mean that the continual use of violence had turned them into naturally violent characters, continually on the look-out for fresh opportunities of violence. No! If you believe that, you have neither suffered nor inflicted real pain. It is my testimony that for the most part the true motive for their actions was a secret, silent, inward, gnawing determination not to have committed crime that achieved no object. In the final analysis these are the actions of damned souls making their last desperate effort to wreak vengeance on the devil who has led them into hell.

'The people of France, in whose name justice is now supposedly being done, should know that it was in their name and for their sake that the accused were pushed, by those in authority, over the edge of this pit of destruction.'

Such a testimony, emotional but nevertheless well-argued, was very different from the kind of evidence usually given. In cases of this sort, and particularly during the 'barricades' trial, the defence always put to both the accused and the witnesses the view that 'false, scandalous' accusations of torture had played a decisive part in the officers' revolt. In this case, however, torture is presented with unimpeachable logic as an extenuating circumstance.* For the first time the shameful conspiracy linking those who gave the order and those who carried it out was exposed. An officer had himself given an explanation of the working of some of the cogs in the machine which I have tried to describe in this book. Naturally we must make some allowance for poetic license in his evidence. All the officers who tortured, or who took part in the various *putschs* were certainly not as sensitive as Captain Estoup's 'young curates'. We must make allowances for certain individuals who, in the situation prevailing in Algeria, were given an opportunity to exercise inherent sadistic tendencies; we may also reasonably ask (which Captain Estoup did not do) why information was such a military necessity and what was

---

* These tactics succeeded, for the officers concerned escaped the death penalty which had, however, been inflicted not long before on one of their fellow-officers, Lieutenant Degueldre, who was another ex-torturer; but, as a leader-writer in *Le Monde* pointed out, he did not have the advantage of being a St Cyr graduate.

to prevent the war in Algeria going on for ever unless it were brought to an end by negotiation. Still the fact remains that no one had hitherto set out so forcibly the tragic consequences of the *political* path chosen by Paris. Serious consideration of the point raised in Captain Estoup's testimony (which was in fact almost entirely squeezed out of the majority of newspapers by other subjects)* might have helped to diagnose and treat the sickness from which France is suffering and which the end of the Algerian war has not yet cured.

The Greek historian Thucydides of Athens, whom I have already quoted, hoped that if, like a good doctor, he could set out the symptoms of the political ills of his age, he would make it easier for future generations to diagnose these symptoms should they recur. The crisis of France may therefore serve to highlight a tragedy which is not that of France alone. We all realize that the practice of torture has spread throughout the world both in strong societies and in those that feel threatened or insecure. Quite apart from Nazi Germany and Fascist Italy, torture was used until the 'de-Stalinization' of the Soviet Union and in the Peoples' Democracies; on 30 June 1960 King Baudouin heard some revealing comments on the character of the Belgian occupation of the Congo from Patrice Lumumba; and several similar examples of the Franco-Algerian tragedy can be seen in the very recent colonial history of the United Kingdom, without going back to the nineteenth-century Irish problem, the 'agrarian crimes' of the Sinn Feiners (so similar to those of the *fellagha*), or to the methods of repression then used. A look at the Cyprus or Kenya crises shows some striking similarities. In both cases an insurrection broke out; in Cyprus it constituted a political challenge to British domination; in Kenya it sprang partly from a peasant population deprived of its land, and with no definite political objective, being led by despair and the social disruption caused by detribalization to use the vilest methods. In both cases it was met by a machine of repression that was largely out of date

* Oddly enough the full text was published and commented upon only in a left-wing weekly, *L'Express*, and in an ultra right-wing daily, *La Nation française*, which, by a complicated piece of reasoning, held that it justified the concept of French Algeria – 'we had to go right through with it'.

and incapable of doing its job. 'The police force had remained almost unchanged, except for a change of title, since 1878,' wrote Lawrence Durrell in his book on Cyrpus, *Bitter Lemons*. The most significant passages in a well-documented but incomplete study, *A Historical Survey of the Origins and Growth of Mau-Mau*, prepared by F. D. Corfield at the request of the Colonial Office, deal with the defects of the Intelligence organization. A political decision had to be made on the extent of repressive action to be undertaken. To the London Government the 40,000 Kenya settlers represented a pressure-group analogous to that of the French of Algeria. In Cyprus outdated considerations of strategy were the governing factor – an agreement to evacuate the Suez base had been reached in 1954, and actual evacuation had followed in 1956. Uncompromising language was used; on 28 July 1958 the Secretary of State for the Colonies, Mr Hopkinson, stated in the House of Commons that British sovereignty in Cyprus would *never* be a matter for discussion.

Fine words and facile explanations followed. The Corfield Report, which was not published until 1960, gives the impression that the British Government believed the baleful influence of Jomo Kenyatta to be largely responsible for the Mau-Mau insurrection. Field-Marshal Harding in Cyprus showed that he held similar views when he said to the Editor of the *Times of Cyprus:*

'Not five per cent of Greek Cypriots are behind this evil organization. Not five per cent! The rest of the population detested EOKA, its brutal deeds and dastardly murders. . . . This was not a patriotic rising, it was the work of fanatics without a following.'*

To deal with these incipient insurrections a complete armoury of legislation was brought into force. A 'state of emergency' was declared in Kenya on 20 October 1952 and in Cyprus on 26 November 1955; detention laws, initially accepted even by the liberal section of the public, made it possible to keep men in prison or in detention camps in spite of the fact that no legal

* See Charles Foley's book *Island in Revolt* (Longmans, London, 1962), which is especially interesting because the author, who was at one time foreign editor of the *Daily Express*, can hardly be accused of violent anti-colonialism.

charge had been brought against them. But, although it was the civil power which drafted the legislation, it was eventually compelled to entrust its execution to the Army. Lawrence Durrell accurately described the situation in *Bitter Lemons:* 'What the police could not enforce, the military would have to undertake at gun point.' The words could equally well have been written to describe the situation in Algiers in 1957.

The machinery of repression that began to turn was true to type. Charles Foley recorded the impressions of his assistant, Michael Davidson:

Michael had seen it all before and could anticipate most of the steps on the road to repression, as pioneered in Malaya by General Sir Gerald Templer. Curfew from dusk to dawn, then a curfew which would keep people in their homes all day as well: a State of Emergency declared: the public finger-printed, identity cards issued: collective fines on towns and villages. Page after page of the 'Templer Bible' was torn out and sent to the Cyprus Government printer. Next day it was law.

And of course, faced with a population which, either willingly or unwillingly, was working with the terrorists, the Army came up against the problem of Intelligence. Although torture never became an institution as it did in Algeria and later in France, it does seem that after the end of 1956 there were British officers in Cyprus who used it, mainly on their own initiative, but probably often covered by their superiors. The legislation passed during the state of emergency made things easier. In Cyprus the period for which a man could be held by the police without appearing before a court was raised from forty-eight hours to sixteen days, and later to twenty-eight days – time enough for any marks of violence to have vanished if necessary.

In Kenya the Cowan Plan, which was intended – probably quite genuinely – to help with the re-education of the hard-core Mau-Mau prisoners by re-introducing them to work, was interpreted and executed by prison administrators and wardens in such a way that, on 3 March 1959, eleven prisoners at Hola Camp were beaten to death.

The system of justice could hardly remain unaffected by such legislation. By trying to achieve exemplary severity, it soon lost in legality and tended to become a mere tool of repression. Several hundred men were hanged in Kenya. In Cyprus the effect on the rapidly worsening situation of the execution of Michael Caraolis and Andreas Demetriou in May 1956 was strikingly similar to that of the first executions in Algiers in June 1956.

Such a system of justice might easily lead the authorities to condone the use of torture, just as the French system had done. To their credit some Cyprus judges, Mr Justice Shaw for instance, refused to accept legal proceedings which seemed to be based on information got by the use of torture. During the early days of the Cyprus revolt two captains were, at the instance of a Turkish magistrate, convicted of having used violence, court-martialled, and cashiered; but there were not many such convictions. In November 1956 the citizens of Cyprus were deprived of the right to institute proceedings against members of the Government or security forces without first having obtained the agreement of the Attorney-General of the colony; this agreement was never forthcoming since the preliminary inquiry was in the hands of the police who were working in close collaboration with the security forces. The same piece of legislation authorized heavy fines on newspapers bold enough to publish texts of complaints before the inquiry concerned had been held. There is nothing to show that in Kenya the real culprits in the Hola Camp affair, that is those who so crassly misinterpreted the admittedly ambiguous recommendations of the Cowan Report, were ever punished, in spite of the detailed nature of the Coroner's inquiry and the courage of the Resident Magistrate.

The question arises whether these practices were encouraged by the existence of a local counter-terrorist organization as in Algeria.

It is clear that the settlers in Kenya were often sorely tempted to take justice into their own hands. In Cyprus, where the British amounted only to an insignificant minority, the problem was complicated by the existence of a sizeable Turkish community who themselves formed an anti-EOKA organization called Volcan. Volcan. The rivalry between these two organizations was sometimes exploited by the authorities. A tragic example will show where this policy might have led if it had been followed further.

In May 1958 nine Greeks were released by the authorities from arrest near the Turkish village of Guenyeli, and were massacred by the villagers. The official report on this affair merely concluded that the security forces had been 'indiscreet' in setting the Greeks free near a place where they were in danger of being set upon by the Turks.

When accusations were made against the forces of law and order in Algeria, the answer was often given that all members of the F.L.N. had orders from their leaders to declare that any confessions they might have made had been obtained by torture. When the British Army came under attack after certain incidents in Cyprus, the same somewhat lame defence was made.

So, as in Algeria, the first steps were taken towards an era of deception. It is interesting to try and see whether a policy of deception began to take root in the civil and military hierarchy, as it did in France. Certainly Mr Macmillan, Mr Julian Amery, and Mr Alan Lennox-Boyd made statements remarkably similar to those of M. Mollet and M. Bourgès-Maunoury. For example, on 24 February 1959, a week before the Hola Camp drama, Mr Amery said:

'The Government of Kenya and the Prison Service in Kenya is perfectly capable of keeping its own house in order and is doing so. Our contention is that the organization of the Prison Service is right and is what it should be and that safeguards against abuse are effective.'

The 'morale' of the Army, both commanders and troops, was at stake. The military authorities could count on many of their men disliking the 'Cyps' and therefore taking a tough line. 'Don't forget,' General Kendrew said one day, 'my twenty-five thousand propagandists at home, the men who've done their tour in Cyprus. I can rely on them to support our case. They're mostly National Servicemen scattered all over the country and what they say's believed.' In fact in September 1958 when Barbara Castle, an ex-Chairman of the Labour Party, had the courage to broach the subject and say in terms that may admittedly have been exaggerated that she believed that the troops were 'permitted and even encouraged' to employ needlessly brutal methods in 'hot pursuit', she was censured and sanctimoniously called to order from all sides, even by the leader of her own party, Mr

Gaitskell. A considerable section of the British left wing more-over accepted a policy of silence in order that public opinion should not be shocked or the morale of the Army affected.

But of course things never went so far as in Algeria and France – for a number of reasons, including, no doubt, the traditional dexterity of the British Government in withdrawing to previously prepared positions.

In Cyprus, if the situation had got worse than it did, it would have jeopardized the whole structure of NATO, of which both Greece and Turkey are members, and the internal order of both these countries. This largely explains the decisive role which the Greek and Turkish governments played in the formulation of an agreement signed at the beginning of 1959. In Kenya, politicians emerged in Britain, more especially the Colonial Secretary, Ian Macleod, who were prepared to evaluate properly the growing force of African nationalism (of which the Kikuyu movement was in most senses a part), and to impose a compromise on the settler population which would, in due course, give the Africans political control of the country. Furthermore, neither Cyprus nor Kenya was bound by such close links to the United Kingdom as Algeria was by economic, social, political, and sentimental bonds to France.

But can anyone say that a deterioration of moral standards like that which afflicted France could not possibly take place on the British side of the Channel, or indeed anywhere else?

Some, when they compare these sets of facts, may conclude that no state and no society can be held responsible for the development of a chain of events which seems to have every attribute of inevitability. But there is another conclusion which may be drawn from these unhappy comparisons – that the fight against torture and the search for the truth must be pursued on an international plane.

This search for truth is precisely what the French government renounced. Five days after the signature of the Évian Agreements, two amnesty decrees were published in the *Journal Officiel* of the French Republic. The first applied to members of the F.L.N. as prescribed in the Évian Agreements; it applied also to men who had received heavy sentences and who had seen many of their comrades executed. The key paragraph of the second decree said: 'An amnesty is also granted for any illegal actions committed before 20 March 1962 resulting from any law-and-order operations undertaken against the Algerian insurrection.' At a stroke of the pen the torturers were acquitted, although they had never been tried. Torture was erased from the record and life went on as if it had never existed. Of course the decision is not surprising. So many of the torturers had been awarded decorations that it would have been much more surprising if any action *had* been taken against them at the end of the war. Nevertheless, the French Government's decision raises a general, one might almost say an international, problem.

An amnesty is an entirely normal feature of the end of a political crisis such as the one which France has just survived. It is a type of measure that has been used in every age and under every régime. There are, for instance, very few ex-collaborators still in prison today in any of the countries once occupied by the Germans; in Ancient Greece, peace-treaties frequently included a clause laying down that those who had been banished on each side should be repatriated; immediately after the French Revolution, those who had been condemned to death and fled were allowed to return, and the prisons were gradually opened; an amnesty was declared for those supporters of the Commune of 1871 who had not been shot by the Versailles Government. Every legal system sets a term both for misdemeanour and for felony. The misdemeanour or felony is held no longer to exist at the end of a defined period which varies according to the crime in question. At the conclusion of this period, the danger to society stemming from the crime is considered no longer to exist. The concluding sentence of Balzac's *Les Chouans* reads: 'In 1827 an old man and his wife were selling cattle in the Fougères market. No one spoke ill of him although he had killed more than a hundred people.'

But the amnesty which put an end to any possible proceedings against the torturers, or rather made such proceedings legally impossible, was something quite different. It set the seal on the hypocritical attitude which the State had always adopted towards this vital problem. It legitimized *a posteriori* actions which the

State had neither been able nor willing to stop. The State had so to speak decreed an amnesty for itself.

The consequences were extremely serious. Thousands of men had been brought to believe in the worst form of violence, violence against an unarmed enemy. They had no feeling of guilt and often dared to boast of their crimes. In any social or political crisis in the future, they will be available as henchmen for any adventurer. The techniques which they learnt in Algeria may be used in other places. Throughout the structure of the nation, throughout the machinery of State, the torturers are there; they are there in the Army, they are there in the police, they are there in the judicial system. Nothing less than the whole future of the French nation is at stake.

The amnesty granted to the torturers may be a serious matter for France, but it is equally serious internationally; it makes nonsense not only of French law but of the Geneva Conventions, the International Declaration on Human Rights, and the Nuremberg Trials. By International Law, any country is entitled to punish a crime against humanity. So if one day persons in the pay of Algeria, or of any other country, kidnap a French torturer and bring him before a regular court of law, this will be neither more nor less of a scandal than the kidnapping and trial of Adolf Eichmann. Nor is this so fanciful a picture as it might seem. United Nations' forces in the Congo have already issued warrants for the arrest of French officers who were notorious for their crimes in Algeria and later became mercenaries in Mr Tshombe's Katanga army. There is truth in Professor Laurent Schwartz's ironic remark: 'France was once the purveyor of culture; she is now the purveyor of torturers.'

The French Government has chosen the wrong solution, for France will one day have to admit that it is unhealthy to leave crime unpunished. But it is much more difficult to say what in justice and fairness ought to have been done. Where does the responsibility for these crimes begin and end? This is, of course, no new problem; it was raised in post-war Germany. But there circumstances were different because Nazism, like all totalitarian systems, had no need to be hypocritical. For instance, the orders for 'Operation Barbarossa' in 1941 were quite open in laying down that: 'There is no obligation to prosecute German soldiers for actions in connexion with enemy civilians, even if these actions constitute crimes.' They were different also because in 1954 most Frenchmen believed Algeria to be an inseparable part of their own country, which, of course, was not the case with the Germans in relation to France, Poland, and the U.S.S.R. Finally, they were different because the Germans were (if we may use the phrase) saved the trouble of trying their own leading war criminals by the willingness of their conquerors to do it for them.

Nevertheless, the German intellectuals felt that they must face this question of war guilt, *die Schuldfrage*. Karl Jaspers wrote the following words (which Éditions de Minuit reproduced on the title page of *La Question*):

The man who sits and does nothing knows in his heart that he is morally guilty. He is guilty each time he fails to answer the call, each time he fails to take advantage of an opportunity of taking some action to protect those threatened, to reduce the sense of injustice and to resist the spread of evil. Even when we were powerless to do other than submit, there was always something that could be done – not without some risk, of course, but provided one was careful one could still achieve something. The man who, through fear, lets some chance of taking action go by, must admit to himself that he is morally guilty; insensitivity in face of the misfortunes of others, lack of real imagination, indifference at heart to misery which leaps to the eye, all this adds up to moral guilt.*

Moral guilt. It would be only too easy to prove that there is much of that in France today, even among those who raised their voices against the practice of torture. The tentacles of the monster spread so wide that no one can feel himself entirely blameless. But there are few things more difficult than to relate moral guilt to legal guilt; the young soldier who turned the handle of the magneto at the orders of his officer, the officer who knew that he was backed up by the civil authorities, the minister who gave orders to pacify Algeria 'by all available means', Parliament which voted special powers when it knew or ought to have known

* Karl Jaspers, *Die Schuldfrage*, 1946.

what use would be made of them: which of these is legally responsible and in what measure? This seems to be a case in which responsibility was so widely spread that it is almost impossible to pin it down.

The only answer to the legal problem is in fact a political one. The torturers, preferably those most directly involved, must be tried, but it hardly seems possible to imprison everybody who directly or indirectly took part in torture. The only possible solution is to brand the torturer with some sort of 'national ignominy'. After the Liberation all members of the Parliament which passed the law delegating power to Marshal Pétain, so leading to the end of the Third Republic, were condemned to 'national ignominy', from which they had to redeem themselves by subsequent good behaviour. The same sentence was pronounced on a number of collaborators whose guilt was a moral one. In the same way it should now be made impossible for anyone known to have been involved in torture to become a deputy or a minister or a police officer or an Army officer.

But it is far more important to decree national ignominy upon the practice of torture than upon individual torturers. This is an infinitely more complex problem. In the first place, it presupposes that we do not deliberately forget the whole episode. This is first and foremost the business of our teachers. Chauvinism must not be used as an excuse for silence. Nothing can be more mistaken than the rule 'my country, right or wrong'. Federal Germany provides a good example of what not to do in such a situation. Little by little the concentration camps, the fearful crimes of Nazism, and the entire Hitler period are disappearing from German history books; first, the books for primary schools were purged; now it is the turn of those for secondary schools. It will not be long before only those taking a course of higher education will even know what the word 'Auschwitz' implies. It was only the Eichmann Trial and the justifiable publicity given to it, which reminded young Germans that National Socialism had dedicated itself to the task of liquidating the Jewish people.

The teachers' organizations therefore have a vital task to carry out in this field; but experience indicates that they are ill-equipped for it. While the Algerian war was still on, they were often begged, by those who cared, to include a period on the evils of torture in the programme of every level of education from the village school to the Sorbonne. It was February 1962 before they brought themselves to do so and as soon as the Minister of Education forbade them to use school buildings for the purpose, the teachers meekly kept quiet and read themselves the lesson intended for their pupils. It is, of course, no easy task. One cannot tell young children everything; after all, the way to begin teaching boys or girls about sex is not to show them pictures of the frightful effects of syphilis! But means can and must be found of producing a mental reaction among the young which associates the idea of torture with a feeling of shame.

Beside this reform in education, there must be a reform of the organization of the State. An obvious first step is the abolition of the military courts and of emergency legislation. It is perfectly proper for a State to prepare some exceptional measures to meet exceptional circumstances should they arise, but it can never, in any circumstances, be right for a man to be put into the power of the police simply by virtue of some legal document. The French penal code lays down that after twenty-four hours under detention every prisoner has the right to be medically examined. This provision was designedly omitted from the regulation dealing with confinement orders, and as a result suspects could be detained in police establishments without supervision of any kind. To let such legislation stand is tantamount to allowing the practice of torture to stand.

Moreover, experience shows that the police only employ brutal methods because they do not know their job. It is a fundamental duty of any democracy to educate its police, pay them adequately, and control them. The police are far too often regarded as the dustmen of society, and if we accept such a divorce of the police from the rest of the community, we are also accepting that the police will lose their self-respect and start to employ shameful methods. Justice is only worthy of the name if it is dispensed openly, is continually checked in the light of public opinion, and looked upon not as a function of the State and its machine of repression but as a public service at the disposal of the user, whoever he may be, and with the power to deal with anybody. But we know that this was not true in France even before the start of the Algerian war. If a man wishes to bring a complaint against a police officer in France, legal action will never be begun by the authorities. According to French law, the victim has to bring a civil case in order to get the law to intervene, and he then soon finds that the standard of proof required to convict a policeman is far higher than that required to convict an ordinary citizen. Nor is police sanctity and impregnability the prerogative of the French alone. The Podola affair and the case of the Nuclear Disarmament demonstrators showed that it is also sometimes enjoyed by the British police.

When a normal system of justice proves ineffective, the State usually has recourse to a more authoritative procedure – that of extraordinary justice. Commissions of inquiry set up by Parliament are, in themselves, an excellent institution. Experience has shown, however, that when the problem is to protect the rights of the individual, a commission of inquiry serves no real purpose if its arguments are kept secret or it merely becomes one more cog in the machinery of the State. When any civil dispute is submitted to arbitration, each side has the right to appoint half the arbitrators; the arbitrators then agree among themselves on the choice of a chairman or senior arbitrator who has a casting vote. This type of procedure might very well be employed to ensure that the rights of the individual are guaranteed.

These proposals may appear commonplace or indeed so simple as to be even ridiculous. Experience, unfortunately, shows that even the simple and obvious solution cannot be guaranteed to succeed. Experience also unfortunately shows that guarantees, however cast-iron they may appear, carry little weight when a certain social class or caste within the State consider that their power or position can only be maintained by the use of torture. Checks and balances can, of course, be devised and put into practice, but in themselves they are no panacea. The use of torture in Algeria was to a great extent the defensive reaction of a minority whose privileged position was threatened, of an army which had been ordered to protect this minority and which could find no other means of action, and of a government which, with the support of the majority of the nation, did all it could over a period of years to ensure that this minority retained its privileged position.

The relationship between the torturers and the tortured was further exacerbated by a spirit of racial prejudice and the contempt for their inferiors of men who considered themselves superior beings. The reason why so many spectators watched the torture of Henri Alleg at El-Biar was because the torturers had the unusual opportunity of torturing one of their own race. As long as the relationships between men are based upon the domination by one race of another or on the colour of a man's skin, the practice of torture will never disappear.

But racialism is not the whole answer either. It was not a feeling of racial superiority which caused the German Nazis to torture other non-Nazi Germans. The Greek City State had the logical answer when it refused to admit that slaves were human beings and therefore considered torture inflicted upon a slave to be a perfectly normal occurrence, whereas inflicted on a free man it became an abominable crime. The essential feature of the practice of torture, therefore, is that one man or one class of society claims absolute power over another man or another class of society. Western society does not in general terms need to have recourse to torture. The 'mass media', the sensational Press and modern publicity techniques, are in normal times quite adequate to allow the ruling classes to keep the peace within a society. Aldous Huxley's *Brave New World* is in many respects a truer and more accurate picture of the goal to which our society is moving than the terrifying world depicted by Orwell. An attempt to get to the bottom of these problems would require another volume and that is another story: but rest well assured that the practice of torture will never disappear until all men have come to possess the qualities which are the true hall-mark of humanity.

Text of the Wuillaume Report

Office of the Governor-General
Civil Inspectorate-General in Algeria
Algiers. 2 March 1955

YOUR EXCELLENCY,

You have been good enough to entrust to me an inquiry into certain acts of violence reported in the Press which were said to have been inflicted by the police on persons arrested as a result of the events of 1 November; you also authorized me to visit and inspect the various establishments used by the police during law and order operations.

I have the honour to report to you on this task.

At the outset I draw attention to the fact that, in view of the disquiet shown by all sections of the police force as a result of:

1. the Press campaign,
2. the strict instructions issued to them that violence was not to be used on pain of severe punishment,
3. above all, the inquiry which I was conducting,

I felt that I should not extend my investigation beyond the Kabylie and the department of Constantine. In any event I consider that I have sufficient information to form a judgement.

If you consider it necessary, Your Excellency, I can continue my inquiry in the departments of Algiers and Oran.

In the department of Constantine and in the Aurès I interrogated a certain number of persons held in penal establishments.

In the prisons at Lambèse, Batna, Guelma, and Constantine, I chose at random a certain number of prisoners, sixty-one in all, and interrogated them, taking care that, as the inquiry proceeded, those who had already been questioned should have no opportunity of coming in contact with those who had still to be dealt with.

These prisoners could not therefore have agreed upon a common line beforehand. Furthermore, none of them could have briefed one of those lawyers of the type to be found in Algiers who are believed to urge their clients to lay complaints against the police and so in some instances lead them to make a case out of figments of the imagination.*

Furthermore several of the prisoners (twenty-one out of sixty-one) stated that no violence had been used on them. As far as the remainder are concerned, the type of violence inflicted on them seemed to differ with each individual and, although one or two forms of violence recur in several statements, these statements do not give the impression of having been rehearsed beforehand.

These statements may therefore fairly be given the benefit of any doubt there may be and in general, apart from one or two possible exaggerations, they appear to be truthful.

In fact certain members of the police force, although emphasizing that they could not officially admit to having used methods forbidden by law, confided to me subsequently on a personal basis that some of the methods denounced by the Press were old-established practice (I refer to these statements here only to support the view I have myself formed); they further stated that the effectiveness of these methods was proved and that, considering the acts of violence which the police must at times necessarily use, they were far less barbaric than others, such as the well-known 'beat-up' method, against which no one protests.

The police force in Algeria does therefore use violence when making arrests and carrying out interrogations. Although it is not possible to deduce the total figure of those subjected to violence from the number of prisoners interrogated by me, it is of interest that forty of these out of sixty-one stated that they had been subjected to violence, in some cases of a serious nature; I consider, therefore, that the total figure

---

* The lawyers particularly referred to (quite unjustly) are Maître Pierre and Maître Renée Stibbe. Claude Bourdet gave details of a number of these cases in *L'Observateur* on 13 January 1955. 'An instructive case was that of Adad Ali who was a member of the Algiers Municipal Council. He was arrested on 27 December. On 30 December his lawyer, Maître Pierre Stibbe, notified the Public Prosecutor that he had not reappeared and had not been brought before a magistrate; he demanded that, in accordance with criminal law, he should immediately either be set free or brought before a magistrate. The Public Prosecutor refused to accede to this request, giving as his reason that 'the police were overworked and exhausted'. On 31 December Mme Adad, who feared for her husband's survival in view of his delicate state of health, brought an action against the Public Prosecutor for aiding and abetting illegal imprisonment. A few hours later Adad Ali was brought before an examining magistrate by five inspectors of the general Intelligence service. The journalists, lawyers, and magistrates present all noted that mentally he seemed completely dazed and physically he was in a shocking condition, numerous marks of blows being visible on him.' (Author's note.)

must be fairly high. On the other hand the Public Prosecutors in Batna and Constantine consider that the number of persons subjected to violence after arrest is probably very small. To support this they say that no case of the use of violence has been brought before the Batna Court and only one before the Constantine Court, which was brought by an individual who had already been under detention for more than three weeks and who acted only under pressure from his lawyer.

The Public Prosecutor in Batna, however, stated further that on his own initiative he had had medically examined more than eighty of the accused persons who had been handed over to him and that none of the medical reports mentioned injuries which could be attributed to violence on the part of the police. Nevertheless note must be taken of the large number of cases brought before the court in Algiers even if the majority were brought on the initiative of lawyers.

I do not suggest that the good faith of these officials should be called in question but I must observe that many forms of violence leave no mark and that, if such marks did exist, the periods of detention in police establishments were generally long enough for them to have disappeared.

Among the twelve prisoners whom I interrogated at Lambèse, however, I found three who will for a long time show signs of the violence to which they had been subjected; one had had the soles of his feet burnt with an alfalfa grass torch; another had a large sore on his instep caused by electrical burns; the third had both shoulders dislocated or at least the muscles of both arms torn (only X-ray examination could show which), having had his arms tied behind his back and then having been strung up by the wrists.

Finally, as in France, there has been in Algeria a change in the respective duties of the examining magistrates and of their assistants, the officers of the criminal police. As a result of the inadequate number of magistrates and the lack of facilities at their disposal (the courts, for instance, have no official vehicles and must use police vehicles; the number of typists available to them is inadequate, etc.), it is in fact the police who prepare the case and who bring the accused before the magistrate together with a sheaf of assumptions, proofs, and confessions to establish his guilt. In practice the examining magistrate does no more than read the indictment and sign the committal order.

But I fear that if the police were allowed to do no more than hunt down and arrest 'suspected culprits', and if it was the job of the examining magistrates to establish their guilt, many crimes and misdemeanours would go unpunished. I do not wish to question the professional integrity of the magistrates but it is possible that, where acts of violence on the part of the police are concerned, they are not sufficiently insistent upon knowing what procedures enable the police to bring before them 'water-tight' cases.

However, although violence was used in many cases during the police action following 1 November 1954, it would seem that many fewer instances have occurred since 15 January, on which date the Prefect of Constantine issued very strict instructions to the police that these practices should cease.

I now propose to deal in turn with:

1. The forms of violence used.
2. The authority under which violence was used.
3. The efficacy in certain circumstances of the use of coercion.

1. The Forms of Violence Used

The following are the forms of violence to which the prisoners whom I interrogated stated that they had been subjected:

1. Imprisonment for periods in excess of twenty-four hours, in some cases up to fifteen or twenty days.

2. Beatings with fists, sticks, or whips.

3. Water method. The person is held under water until he is practically suffocated or has even lost consciousness.

4. Water-pipe method. A tube similar to a piece of gas piping is connected to a tap, or failing that a jerrican or other container. The victim's wrists and ankles are tied with his arms and legs bent and he is so held that his elbows are slightly below his knees; a thick stick is then passed between elbows and knees. Once he is thus trussed up, he is rolled backwards on to an old tyre or inner tube where he is firmly wedged. His eyes are bandaged, his nose stopped up, the tube thrust into his mouth, and water passed through it until he is practically suffocated or loses consciousness.

5. Electrical method. Two electric leads are connected to the mains and their bare ends applied like red-hot needles to the most sensitive parts of the body such as armpits, neck, nostrils, anus, penis, or feet. Alternatively the two wires are wound one round each ear or one round each ankle or one round a finger and the other round the penis. If mains electricity is not available, the field electrical supply is used or the batteries of the signals W/T sets.

6. Other forms of violence. One prisoner stated that he had been interrogated while tied to a table in such a way that his head was hanging over the edge. Another stated that after arrest he had been strung up by the feet and that the soles of his feet had been burnt by a torch

made of alfalfa grass; he actually showed me two large scars on the soles of his feet.

Two prisoners stated that they had been strung up by their arms which were tied behind their backs; one of them, who must have been pulled up too high, had had his shoulders dislocated, or at any rate the muscles of his arms torn. He is slowly getting better but his fellow-prisoners still have to feed him.*

Another prisoner stated that two longish pieces of wood had been tied on either side of his head and the two ends projecting above his head had then been struck with a cane. The resulting shock to the skull and brain was such, that according to him, he would soon have been driven mad.

Yet another stated that he had been compelled to stand for four consecutive days and nights, being unable either to sit or lie since his arm was fastened at full stretch to the ceiling.

Finally in the Kabylie, if not elsewhere, persons were forced to dance naked in front of their relatives and neighbours, which for a Muslim is a fearful humiliation, worse than most forms of physical violence.

2. The Authority under which Violence was Used

All parts of the police force – the gendarmerie, the criminal police, and the general information service, made more or less general use during interrogations of beatings-up, the water and water-pipe method, and the electrical method; in general terms the water-pipe method seems, to judge from the frequency with which it was used, to be the one usually preferred.

In the department of Constantine the general information service made use of these methods only to a very limited extent owing to the very unsuitable nature of the quarters which they had available (usually a few offices – sometimes only two – in a prefecture or sub-prefecture); but if necessary, it used the 'establishments' of other sections of the police. The general information service seems to have been the only section which compelled Muslims to dance naked; at any rate in Kabylie this was known as the 'general information service interrogation'.

It is extremely difficult to fix the responsibility for the use of violence even in the most serious cases. To begin with, it is practically impossible to prove that the water method, water-pipe method, or electrical method have been used, since they leave no marks. The criminal police are primarily involved here and naturally they vigorously deny that they

* One wonders how the examining magistrate and the court explained away the condition of the accused in this case. (Author's note.)

have ever used such methods; the fact that there may be a tap and an old tyre or an electric point near a prison where a prisoner says they are, does not prove that the suspect was trussed up, rolled on to the tyre, and had his mouth connected to the tap by a piece of piping. Moreover, a member of the criminal police explained to me confidentially that they are expert at using these methods without endangering the victim's life and that they only bring before the magistrates persons who are 'in good shape' and on whom no medical examination could find any marks of the violence to which they may have been subjected.

There remains the question of those forms of violence which do leave some mark, and particularly the worst of them which, according to the prisoners, were generally used by the gendarmerie. Since I limited my inquiry to the department of Constantine, the majority of the gendarmerie posts against which complaints were made were those in or near the Aurès and this, when the majority of the arrests were made, was an operational area. The barracks concerned housed not only the gendarmerie but also units of the Army, *garde mobile*, and C.R.S. [security companies]; there were also reserve gendarmes mobilized from the European population who made no secret of their opinion that the native population does not appreciate being kindly treated. In some cases violence was used in the mountains, on the spot where the arrest was made (this was the case with the 'suspect' who was strung up by the ankles and had the soles of his feet burnt). Prisoners whom I interrogated said that 'men in uniform' beat them up with rifle butts. No doubt if prolonged and detailed inquiries were undertaken, it would in some instances be possible to name those responsible for particularly serious cases of the use of violence, but these inquiries would encounter very serious difficulties.

It is not my purpose to make excuses or put forward extenuating circumstances for the worst of these excesses, but the following facts should be borne in mind:

1. The atrocities committed by the terrorists themselves: they massacred or mutilated large numbers of their fellow-countrymen suspected of remaining loyal to France; within a period of three months and in the district of Arris alone, where the population is not solely Muslim, fourteen Muslims were murdered, ten vanished without trace, four were mutilated (nose cut off, ear cut off, nails torn out), and four were brutally beaten up (one had his skull fractured).

2. The number of military personnel or members of the security forces who were killed or wounded in operations against the terrorists. In Aurès thirty-five military personnel, including nine officers and N.C.O.s, had been killed in action by 16 February, and fourteen had been killed

through accidents connected with operations – a total of forty-nine. During the same period there were forty-seven wounded, in varying degrees of severity.

3. All ranks of the police gave of their best after 1 November. They did not spare their energy and they disregarded danger; they made an immense effort, working tirelessly day and night and making light of their exhaustion. Such devotion to duty should receive due recognition.

4. The results achieved are remarkable; maquis were in some cases completely destroyed (e.g. at Medjez-Sfa) or broken up (e.g. at Condé-Smendou); many dangerous terrorists were arrested; practically all active terrorists were identified; numerous caches of arms and explosives were seized, etc.

5. The methods used are old-established; in normal times they are only employed on persons against whom there is a considerable weight of evidence of guilt and for whom there are therefore no great feelings of pity. The present wave of indignation has been that much more acute because arrests were very numerous and were frequently made without due consideration; as a result a considerable proportion of those arrested were able to proclaim their innocence, either because no charge against them could be proved or because they were in fact innocent. Further, the police necessarily had to act quickly and as a result were driven to rely to a great extent on a process of extracting immediate confessions in order to get the maximum amount of information in the minimum possible time.

Some of the forms of violence used are unacceptable but some of the reports of results are first-class.* I do not wish to suggest that the latter justify the former, but in present circumstances I consider that to cast aspersions upon a body of public servants who have so much devotion and indeed so much heroism to their credit, would be unwise and might lead to serious consequences. In my view, therefore, no attempt should be made to pin responsibility on individuals.

3. The Efficacy in Certain Circumstances of the Use of Coercion

Ought we nevertheless to continue to accept the procedures described above?

It goes without saying that all physical violence verging upon torture must be prohibited; this includes the well-known 'beat-up' procedure which can lead to lasting injuries such as ecchymosis, fractures, burns,

* On the copy I saw, instead of '*états de services*' (reports of results) the typist had put '*états de sévices*' (reports of torture). (Author's note.)

etc.; equally all mental violence, which relies on publicly humiliating a person, must be prohibited, for instance compelling Muslims to appear naked in front of their families or to engage in unnatural acts.*

It is equally intolerable that members of the police should make use of their powers of coercion [detention] in order to carry out acts of violence such as whipping or to satisfy some personal grudge; cases of this were reported to me at Bougie and Djidjelli and, it should be noted, have been followed by legal action.

On the other hand are there among the various possible forms of violence some which are essential if the police is to do its job satisfactorily?

There are certain police practices which, although generally accepted, are nevertheless tantamount to violence. Instances are: a prolonged interrogation which relies for its results on the physical exhaustion of the prisoner; refusal to allow the prisoner food, drink, and tobacco, while superintendents and inspectors smoke, drink, and eat in front of him; or merely threats and intimidation.

Those police officers, who were willing to talk to me openly, assured me that, in countries where the ordinary man shows such extraordinary resistance to all types of hardship, the above procedures would have no more effect than simply hitting the man. On the other hand the water and electricity methods, provided they are carefully used, are said to produce a shock which is more psychological than physical and therefore do not constitute excessive cruelty.

According to the 'experts' the correct way of employing the waterpipe method is to introduce water into the mouth up to the point of near-suffocation but not to that of loss of consciousness or filling of the stomach; with the electricity method the correct way is to administer a large number of short shocks as if using a red-hot needle.

I myself am in no position to assert that these practices were effective and am compelled to rely on the statements of those who assured me

---

* M. Benbahmed, Deputy for Constantine, sent me on a letter which had been passed to him by a prisoner; this said that when the prisoner was arrested together with his nephew, members of the gendarmerie and C.R.S. had tried to bring about an unnatural relationship between the two men. I interrogated this prisoner in the prison at Constantine where he was held; he gave me to understand that, since he could not write, he had got a fellow-prisoner who was literate to draft the letter but that he did not agree with its contents, which were untrue. When confronted with the writer of the letter, who denied having made it up, the prisoner stated that the general sense of the letter was misleading. This peculiar attitude throws some doubt on the truth of the account. (Note by R. Wuillaume.)

of this and who, it should be noted, were highly thought of by their superiors.

I would merely point out that, according to certain medical opinion which I was given, the water-pipe method, if used as outlined above, involves no risk to the health of the victim. This is not the case with the electrical method which does involve some danger to anyone whose heart is in any way affected.

If it is agreed that either of these methods produce results and that, as the police say, they would be severely handicapped without them, must we accept them pending the introduction into our legal system of the lie detector and the use of pentothal?*

I am inclined to think that these procedures can be accepted and that, if used in the controlled manner described to me, they are no more brutal than deprivation of food, drink, and tobacco, which has always been accepted.

If this be so, we must have the courage to take action on this difficult problem. Either we must adhere to the hypocritical attitude which has been the rule up to the present, which consists in turning a blind eye to what the police are doing, provided that no signs of the cruelties administered remain and nothing can be proven; although this may cause excesses from time to time, the police would carry on with their own job with the authorities as tacit accomplices. Or alternatively we must assume an attitude of false indignation and pretend that we have been deceived, heap anathema on the heads of the police, forbid any methods of interrogation other than those which are strictly legal, and thereby plunge the police into a state of disorder and paralysis.

But neither of these two approaches is now feasible; the first is untenable because the veil has already been lifted and public opinion is aware of what is happening; the second is untenable because, especially in present circumstances, Algeria must have a more than ordinarily efficient police force. There is only one way of restoring the confidence and drive of the police – to recognize certain procedures and to cover them with authority. At this point, however, a distinction must be drawn between the three sections of the police force.

The general information service should be restricted to obtaining information and should use no inducements other than financial. As far as the gendarmerie is concerned, it should do no more than make arrests and carry on interrogations to establish the identity of the suspect; if it

* It cannot be proved that Captain Chevrel of the Army Medical Service used pentothal on Alleg, as we only have Alleg's word that he was drugged, evidence to my mind true, but which the doctor denied (although he brought no evidence for defamation of character), (Author's note.)

so happens, it should be able to record such other useful items of information as may be given voluntarily. For these two sections the problem is therefore simple. They should be completely and formally forbidden to use violence of any sort.

On the other hand the criminal police, and only the criminal police, should be authorized, on the orders of superior authority and pending the introduction of the lie detector and of pentothal, to use special methods which should be laid down in detail and employed only in the presence of an officer or superintendent of the criminal police.

This conclusion, which takes us back to a recent and painful past, may appear repugnant. But since the problem is with us, we must face it.

I cannot over-emphasize that, in view of the grave danger of the situation in Algeria, it is essential, and indeed vital, that the utmost energy be employed in hunting down and punishing the criminals.

The police have worked well since 1 November, but they are now completely confused and cannot understand why they should be criticized for using long-established methods to achieve their present results. The regular police do not in any case approve of abuses when, as has sometimes been the case, they amount to torture. It is accordingly advisable to ensure that every man knows exactly what is allowed and what is not.

Further, since any excesses committed by the police have already been duly censured, it would be advisable, in order to prove to them that their actions and their devotion to duty have not been misinterpreted, to repay some of them with rewards or letters of congratulation.

This will help to bring about a resumption of activity on the part of the police, which must take place as a matter of urgency; it is inexcusable that in a department such as Constantine, where so many criminals have still to be identified and arrested, the daily-activity reports from all sections of the criminal police on some days simply stated: 'Nothing to report.' Such a situation cannot be allowed to continue.

Conclusions

As a result of this inquiry, which covered Kabylie and the department of Constantine only, I am in a position to state that there is some basis of truth in the articles in the Press dealing with violence inflicted by the police on persons under arrest.

1. Violence has been used; in certain instances this was most serious, amounting to real torture. The general information service, the criminal police, and the gendarmerie have all used these methods, but it would appear that the most serious cases have occurred on gendarmerie prem-

ises or during the arrest of persons to be brought before the gendarmerie. This is not to say that the gendarmes were more prone to use torture than their colleagues in the other security forces; but it was in and around the gendarmerie barracks and establishments in the operational area of Aurès that the amateur policemen congregated, i.e. reservist gendarmes, C.R.S., *gardes mobiles*, or military personnel; these were unable to distinguish between brutality and true police methods and their brutality was accentuated by the ill-temper to which the dangers and hardships of active service gave rise.

2. Any attempt to pin responsibility on individuals is a most difficult matter. Moreover I consider this is not the moment to try. Against the use of violence, which in some cases is long-established practice, must be set the devotion to duty shown by the police, the super-human efforts they have made, and the results they have achieved. Some of the forms of violence used are unacceptable but some of the reports of results are first-class.

I do not wish to suggest that the latter justifies the former, but in present circumstances I consider that to cast aspersions upon a body of public servants, who have so much devotion and indeed so much heroism to their credit, would be unwise and might lead to serious consequences.

3. We must remove the screen of hypocrisy surrounding these police 'procedures'. Only in this way can we restore to the police that confidence which they must have if they are to do their job.

Algeria must at the present time have a more than ordinarily efficient police force. The efficiency of the police depends upon their being able to use certain 'methods'. Authority must therefore back up those police who will be using these methods; they should be used only under certain conditions (on the authority of an officer or superintendent of the criminal police) and authority to use them should be given to the criminal police alone.

Apart from this, and on the assumption that the criminal police in Algeria will be reinforced, all other sections of the police should be strictly forbidden to use any method which amounts to violence.

At the same time, since such excesses as have taken place have been pilloried, it would be advisable to prove to certain police officers that the value of their work is recognized by giving them rewards or letters of congratulation.

> I have the honour to be,
> Your Excellency,
> Your devoted and respectful servant,
> (signed) R. WUILLAUME
> *Civil Inspector-General*

BIBLIOGRAPHY

Henri Alleg, *La Question* (published with *Une Victoire* by Jean-Paul Sartre), Éditions de Minuit, Paris, 1958. *The Question*, John Calder, London, 1958.

Djamal Amrani, *Le Témoin*, Éditions de Minuit, Paris, 1958.

Georges Arnaud and J. Vergès, *Pour Djamila Bouhired*, Éditions de Minuit, Paris, 1958.

Comité Maurice Audin, *Sans Commentaire* (Colonel's Argoud's testimony at the 'barricades' trial), 1961.

Simone de Beauvoir and Gisèle Halimi, *Djamila Boupacha*, Gallimard, Paris, 1961. André Deutsch, London, 1962.

Mohammed Bedjaoui, *La Révolution algérienne et le droit*, International Lawyers Association, Brussels, 1961.

Edward Behr, *The Algerian Problem*, Penguin Books, Harmondsworth, 1961.

Abdel Kader Belhadj, Bechir Boumaza, Moussa Khebaili, and Benaissa Souami, *La Gangrène*, Éditions de Minuit, Paris, 1959. *Gangrene*, John Calder, London, 1960.

Peter Benenson, *Persecution 1961*, Penguin Books, Harmondsworth, 1961.

Robert Bonnaud, *Itinéraire*, Éditions de Minuit, Paris, 1962.

Merry and Serge Bromberger, *Les Treize Complots du treize mai*, Arthème Fayard, Paris, 1958.

Merry and Serge Bromberger with Georgette Elgey and Jean-François Chauvel, *Les Trois Complots du treize mai*, Arthème Fayard, Paris, 1961.

Georges Buis, *La Grotte*, Julliard, Paris, 1961.

Maurice Courrégé, Jacques Vergès, and Michel Zavrian, *Le Droit et la colère*, Éditions de Minuit, Paris, 1960. *Les Disparus* (postscript by Pierre Vidal-Naquet), La Cité, Lausanne, 1959.

J.-M. Darboise, M. Heynaud, and J. Martel, *Officiers en Algérie*, Maspéro, Paris, 1960.

Robert Davèzies, *Le Front*, Éditions de Minuit, Paris, 1959.

R. P. Louis Delarue, *Avec les paras du 1er R.E.P. et du 2me R.P.*, Nouvelles Éditions Latines, Paris, 1962.

Frantz Fanon, *L'An V de la révolution algérienne*, Maspéro, Paris, 1959. *Les Damnés de la terre*, Maspéro, Paris, 1961.

Noël Favrelière, *Le Désert à l'aube*, Éditions de Minuit, Paris, 1960.

BIBLIOGRAPHY

Favrod, Charles Henri, *Le F.L.N. et l'Algérie*, Plon, Paris, 1962.

Xavier Grall, *La Génération du djebel*, Éditions du Cerf, Paris, 1962.

Philippe Héduy, *Au Lieutenant des Taglaïts*, La Table Ronde, Paris, 1961.

Colette and Francis Jeanson, *L'Algérie hors-la-loi*, Éditions du Seuil, Paris, 1956.

Francis Jeanson, *Notre Guerre*, Éditions de Minuit, Paris, 1960.

Hafid Keramane, *La Pacification*, La Cité, Lausanne, 1960.

Jean Lartéguy, *Les Centurions*, Presses de la Cité, Paris, 1961. *The Centurions*, Hutchinson, London, 1961. *Les Prétoriens*, Presses de la Cité, Paris, 1961.

Pierre Leulliette, *Saint-Michel et le dragon*, Éditions de Minuit, Paris, 1961.

André Mandouze, *La Révolution algérienne par les textes*, Maspéro (3rd ed.), Paris, 1962.

François Maspéro, *Le Droit à l'insoumission*, Maspéro, Paris, 1961.

Maurienne, *Le Déserteur*, Éditions de Minuit, Paris, 1960.

Alec Mellor, *La Torture* (2nd ed.), Mame, Paris, 1961.

Thomas Oppermann, *Die algerische Frage*, Kohlhammer Verlag, Stuttgart, 1959.

Claude Paillat, *Dossier secret de l'Algérie*, Le Livre Contemporain, Paris, 1961.

Gérard Périot, *Deuxième classe en Algérie*, Flammarion, Paris, 1962.

Jules Roy, *La Guerre d'Algérie*, Julliard, Paris, 1960.

J.-J. Servan-Schreiber, *Lieutenant en Algérie*, Julliard, Paris, 1957. *Lieutenant in Algeria*, Hutchinson, London, 1958.

Pierre-Henri Simon, *Contre la torture*, Éditions du Seuil, Paris, 1957.

Germaine Tillon, *Les Ennemis complémentaires*, Éditions de Minuit, Paris, 1960.

Jean-Raymond Tourneaux, *Secrets d'État*, Plon, Paris, 1960.

Colonel Roger Trinquier, *La Guerre moderne*, La Table Ronde, Paris, 1961.

Pierre Vidal-Naquet, *L'Affaire Audin*, Éditions de Minuit, Paris, 1958. *La Raison d'état*, Éditions de Minuit, Paris, 1962.

Werth, Alexander, *The De Gaulle Revolution*, Robert Hale, London, 1960.

Many articles, some of great importance, have appeared in daily and weekly papers (*Le Monde*, *France-Observateur*, *L'Express*, *France nouvelle*), also in monthly reviews (*Esprit*, *Les Temps modernes*, *La Nouvelle Critique*, *Vérité-Liberté*, *Témoignages et documents*, *Perspectives socialistes*, *Les Cahiers de la République*).

BIBLIOGRAPHY

Patrick Kessel's articles 'Le Pouvoir civil, l'armée et la torture' (*Temps modernes*, August–September 1960) are especially important, as are those of Laurent Schwartz 'Le Problème de la torture dans la France d'aujourd'hui' (*Les Cahiers de la République*, November 1961).

The books quoted above by Thomas Oppermann and Pierre Vidal-Naquet (particularly *La Raison d'état*) contain detailed bibliographies.

*Some other Penguin Specials
are described on the
following pages*

COMMON SENSE ABOUT SMOKING

C. M. Fletcher, Harvey Cole, Lena Jeger, and Christopher Wood

S213

Every 25 minutes somebody in Great Britain dies of lung cancer. The report of the Royal College of Physicians recently showed an unmistakable connexion between cigarette smoking and this terrible disease.

In this book Dr Fletcher, the secretary of the Royal College of Physicians committee on smoking and air pollution which produced the report *Smoking and Health*, gives a concise account of all the available medical evidence. Mr Cole, an economist, asks and answers such questions as: how much do we spend on cigarettes? Does the Government depend on tobacco tax? Mrs Lena Jeger discusses such social aspects of the problem as how our young people can be helped over the convention that the cigarette is a natural extension of the human face. Finally, some methods of fighting the habit are described by Dr Wood, who directs a non-smokers' clinic at the Central Middlesex Hospital.

In Britain four times as many people die every year of lung cancer as are killed on the roads. It is high time we applied some common sense to smoking.

UNITED NATIONS:
PIETY, MYTH, AND TRUTH

Andrew Boyd

S214

Recently the United Nations Organization has come under heavy fire. Stigmatized as a dangerous runaway that must be checked, strained by its involvement in the Congo, shaken by the mysterious death of Hammarskjöld and by Khrushchev's 'troika' campaign, and now financially in the red, the organization can too easily be represented as a bad risk.

But U.N.O. has evolved in unforeseen ways and many people are entirely ignorant of its true nature. Behind the long and inconclusive debates much hard business is in fact done off-stage, where agreements are shaped to implement action by the world executive which has quietly emerged around the figures of Trygve Lie, Dag Hammarskjöld, and U Thant.

In this Penguin Special Andrew Boyd traces the growth of this executive power over the years since the San Francisco Conference of 1945, by way of Korea, Suez, Lebanon, and Laos to the latest flash-point of Katanga. U.N.O.'s record in politics provides powerful ammunition for the author's final plea for commitment to the world organization. If we are to escape from the nuclear rat-race we must drop our split-minded attitudes and embrace the need for active intervention by the United Nations.

BRITAIN IN THE SIXTIES
HOUSING

Stanley Alderson

S211

Inadequate homes tend to breed insecure families. Slums, cramped quarters, and life-long mortgages bear down on mental and physical health, moral standards, and even education.

This Penguin Special lays out a detailed and critical survey of Britain's housing today. It discloses that slums are being created faster than they are being cleared; that gross anomalies occur in the working of subsidies, and that the removal of Schedule A Tax will increase these; that private tenants, less and less protected by rent control, are in the worst situation of all.

Among Stanley Alderson's targets are the instability of land values, the outmoded methods of numerous builders, and the property racketeers who trade on the needs of the homeless. He makes a strong case for fiscal and legislative remedies which could and should be applied at once.

BRITAIN IN THE SIXTIES
THE FAMILY AND MARRIAGE

Ronald Fletcher

S210

Pulpits, rostrums, and the more deeply entrenched batteries of press and radio resound with lamentations about the decay of family life in Britain. Immorality, divorce, and delinquency stalk the land ... or so we are told.

Is there any truth in this murky picture? Or, on the contrary, do the facts quietly pronounce that the family is more stable today than ever in history? For history, when we survey all classes impartially, is a long tale of poverty, drudgery, desertion, and vagrancy.

In this systematic analysis of the subject, a sociologist discusses the extraordinary coherence of the family group in the face of social changes and provides answers to questions which are often anxiously posed to us: are too many married women working in industry? Is delinquency increasing alarmingly? Has discipline within the family utterly disappeared, or is today's relationship between father and children a new and fuller one? Have teenagers really so much money to spend? And, even if this is so, is it so deplorable?

HAS MAN A FUTURE?

Bertrand Russell

S206

What spurs a famous philosopher, at the age of 89, to plunge into a political campaign of civil disobedience and to go to prison for his beliefs? The answer is an urgent concern for the continuance of the human race.

In the million years during which man has lived on this planet, he must have survived many hazards. Can he hope to survive a nuclear war? Here lies the most agonizing question of our era.

Refuting the theory that scientists have been the willing tools of governments, Bertrand Russell exposes the hypocrisy of official attitudes to nuclear weapons. The one hope for man, he proclaims, is to be found in world government. He maps out a reasoned scheme in this book, and details the practical steps we can take towards it today.

This moving pronouncement – in its admiration of man's past achievements, in the despair engendered by his present plight, in its unquenchable concern for those who follow – is no less than Bertrand Russell's living testament to mankind.

PERSECUTION 1961

Peter Benenson

S200

Persecution 1961 contains nine case studies of persecution, intoler-ance, and brutality in the divided world of the mid-century. Each case shows what can happen to people living under any system of government and law whose views are unacceptable to their rulers or unpopular with their neighbours. The disappearance of Olga Ivinskaya and the imprisonment of Constantin Noica are matched on the other side of the ideological fence by the savage persecution of the Rev. Ashton Jones in America and the appalling humiliation for France of the torture and death of Maurice Audin.

If the worth of human life (dressed in whatever colour of skin) is still to be measured in terms of individual freedom under the rule of a just law, then the price of that freedom is still eternal vigilance, and through Audin's fate, the imprisonment of Patrick Duncan, the flogging of Neto, and indeed all the case studies presented here, *Persecution 1961* shows the classic warning to be an urgent and inescapable task of our time.